Arcimbold(
New and Se

C000177111

Twice shortlisted for the T.S. Eliot prize, Tim Liardet is the recipient of many literary awards and *Arcimboldo's Bulldog: New and Selected Poems* is his eleventh book of poems. Liardet was born in London, educated at the University of York, and worked variously and travelled widely before moving into higher education. He has reviewed contemporary poetry for an extensive number of journals and newspapers, including the *Guardian, Poetry Review* and *PN Review,* and his poetry has been translated into Farsi, Macedonian and German. He has judged many competitions, not least for the Poetry Society, run workshops for the *Guardian,* taught a wide diversity of specialist courses for the Arvon Foundation, for various festivals and institutions in the United States and, from 2016 to 2018, was a Poetry Book Society selector. He has performed his work on BBC Radio Three and BBC Radio Four and at many major festivals and venues, including the Ars Interpres Festival, Stockholm, the Internationales Literaturfestival Berlin, the Royal Festival Hall, Cambridge Public Library in Boston, the KGB bar and other locations in New York, plus a range of different venues in New Hampshire, Maine and Pennsylvania. He is Professor of Poetry at Bath Spa University.

TIM LIARDET

Arcimboldo's Bulldog
New and Selected Poems

CARCANET

First published in Great Britain in 2018 by
Carcanet Press Ltd
Alliance House, 30 Cross Street
Manchester M2 7AQ
www.carcanet.co.uk

A CIP catalogue record for this book is available from the British Library.
ISBN 978 1 784105 70 9

The publisher acknowledges financial assistance from Arts Council England.

Typeset in England by XL Publishing Services, Exmouth
Printed and bound in England by SRP Ltd, Exeter

for Jennifer

Contents

from *The Storm House* (2011)

from *Madame Sasoo Goes Bathing* (2011)

from *The World Before Snow* (2015)

Acknowledgements

Acknowledgements are due to the editors of the following magazines, journals, newspapers and anthologies in which some of these poems first appeared: *Agenda, Ambit, Arts Council England Writers' Awards 2003, Best British Poetry 2012, The Forward Book of Poetry 1995, The Forward Book of Poetry 2007, The Forward Book of Poetry 2008, The Forward Book of Poetry 2012, The Dalhousie Review, The Guardian, The Independent, The Independent on Sunday, London Review of Books, The Malahat Review, The Manhattan Review, The New Republic, New Statesman, Oxford Poetry, PN Review, The Poetry Book Society Anthology, Poetry Durham, Poetry International, Poetry Ireland Review, Poetry London, Poetry London Newsletter, Poetry Review, The Poetry Review, Poetry Wales, The Rialto, Salt Magazine, Slate Magazine, Stand Magazine, Southwest Review, The Spectator, The Times Literary Supplement, The Sunday Times, Thumbscrew, The London Magazine, London Magazine, New Writing 8, New Writing 10, New Writing 11, New Writing 12, The North, Wascana Review, The Warwick Review.*

Acknowledgment is made to Seren for permission to reprint the poems in this book which first appeared in *Fellini Beach, Competing with the Piano Tuner, To the God of Rain* and *The Blood Choir.* Acknowledgement is made to Shoestring Press for permission to reprint the poems in this book which first appeared in *Priest Skear* and *Madame Sasoo Goes Bathing.*

As a collection-in-progress *The Blood Choir* (or rather fourteen of the poems contained in it) won an Arts Council England Writers' Award in April 2003. *For the Seven Hundred and Forty Ninth Species of Barbed Wire, The Language School, The Uses of Pepper* and *The Blood Choir* appeared in the anthology which resulted from that award. I am very grateful for the Hawthornden Fellowship (April-May, 2002) during the expansive space of which *To the God of Rain* was completed and *The Blood Choir* developed. *Competing with the Piano Tuner* was a Poetry Book Society Special Commendation for Summer 1998, and long-listed for the Whitbread Poetry Prize. *To the God of Rain* was a Poetry Book Society Recommendation for Spring 2003. *The Blood Choir* won an Arts Council England Writer's Award as a collection-in-progress, was a winner in the Smith/Doorstop Pamphlet Competition, was a Poetry

Book Society Recommendation for Summer 2006 and shortlisted for the 2006 T.S. Eliot Prize. 'The Law of Primogeniture' was nominated for a Pushcart Prize, November 2008; sections 3, 4, 13 and 19 of 'The Storm House' were nominated for a Pushcart Prize, November 2009. *Priest Skear* was the Poetry Book Society Pamphlet Choice for Winter 2010. *The World Before Snow* was shortlisted for the 2015 T.S. Eliot Prize. 'The World's First Photograph' was nominated for a Pushcart Prize, November 2017.

Thirty of the poems included in this book can be heard on the National Poetry Archive, www.poetryarchive.org

Thank you to Jennifer Militello for shaking up all my preconceptions into a new order.

The question whether our minds are instruments of knowledge, and, if so, in what sense, is so vital that any suggested analysis of mind must be examined in relation to this question. To ignore this question would be like describing a chronometer without regard to its accuracy as a time-keeper, or a thermometer without mentioning the fact that it measures temperature.

Bertrand Russell, *The Analysis of Mind*, 1922

New Poems

On Returning from a Trip to West Virginia The Father Brings his Daughter a Jar of White Lightning
or *Sicilian-American Tough Love*

'...All I got was this lousy moonshine,' you say,
but something in that clear-standing liquefaction
magnified by the curvature of its jar
talked of intimacy as a mischief, an in-joke;
it was a nod to yes as much as nod to no,
a blessing to moody, monstrance to happy;
assent to you as son, as much to you as daughter.
Less than thirty days old, the moonshine dreaming
the tank of some hillbilly bucket of rust
jacked up on bricks with catchweed for blinds,
was as limpid as ether, forty percent pure;
it was as ominous as the devil's bathtub gin,
its depths of ions sparkled, its gases rose,
explained by spilt light. World, be pleased
with what you throw. Amazonian tribesmen,
warily, wade the river to be offered gifts.
A trio of craters gaping a hundred meters wide
surfaces, in North Siberia. And here is love
in its plainest state, securing its vapours
with a screw-thread, marked at eighty proof.

Cop Convo, Subtitles Only

This is my road, says the cop, this the next bend yawning.
This is my road that goes on and on.
I can swing around my long lazy Buick any time I choose
and come after you. I can do what I want.

You act like you do what you choose, she says, like this
is your road. This the immaculate camber
from which you scrape the squashed skunk.
You sweep, you scrape. You need to keep it swept.

I pull you over, he says, you have on your fog-lamps
and there is no fog. Those filaments hot with brilliance
while all your other lights are off, though it is dark.
Most people keep on their lights in the dark.

Most people, she says, keep on all their lights.
I prepare always for an arcane weather.
The particles of darkness are another sort of fog. I probe
another sort of dark. You do not know which sort.

This, he says, is my lamp's blue hysteria, encased in a bottle,
it is the light which beats harder the more I catch up.
Law, she says, is what burns the night blue,
our faces bluer. I wish your fog-lamps fog.

The World's First Photograph

Genesee River, 1890

Coax her out, said the men, from under that hat
where her thoughts are embodied as forty-inch braids
of which she will not yield to pride a single hair.
Offer rum, a jade ear-ring, to teach her the box-
for-stealing-light is not a portal to the next world.
Lead her from her threshold to the weathered
albedo which is her prideful countenance.

Every word of praise a sliver of mirror laid
flat to make a whole mirror. You are, they said,
the baggy-brimmed prophet of the Seneca and must not
begrudge futurity its halo. They fed her

cube after cube of sugar, more rum, until she sat
to stare out fear and have it look away
throughout the century-long exposure, still as stone.

*

As if fear were a chemical, or fear and refusal
in equal measure mixed with steams of bromine
and acted as a soluble. As if the dark hangings
and upholstery's warp yarn had risen through her
or were struck upon another frequency.

As if fear, the chemical, mixed with the fumes
of iodine and mercury and became one vapour
and all that showed up on the plate
was the ghost of a chair, bare of her barest trace.

As if the chair bore the shape of a vague presence
sitting in it, but was as moonless
as a moonless night. As if its carved claw-feet

gripped, gripped to hold in place only the spirit-image
of her tiny feet a little off the ground.

American Rainstorm as Altarpiece

Emboldener of the bulb,
for this raw imminence, gratitude.
Storm, each phase of your sulk
seems to have hijacked one
of our three windows, light to left

and grey to right, black core at centre.
Glass had to be invented once
these rivulets of rain were. All three of you
crowd the centrepiece at last.
You are charcoal that smokes, that burns

however wet it is. The tall centre
rolls up all your ardent darknesses –
it could be the light of Golgotha,
its creepy-crawly billow of soot
like a clouding of insecticide

against the shallowing out of which
you mutter softly to yourself.
First, a getting used to three. Then
the hinges open on one.
Forgive us. We watch. We talk

with hushed, reverent voice
behind one window. Soon, you'll be gone.
The engine of the world
is reducing compression
to tame you. Cyclone, cloud-crawler,

shoveller of the tall hotel
and of everything in its path,
maker of new light, new air, new us,
above the brightening brake lights
on the road climbing north.

Uncanoonuc Whose Cirrus of Light

I'd say the twelfth floor of twelve lost radio contact.
We were too high up, height-to-height with the mountain.
I would say the room belonged to the mountain
in the fetch of which it looked. I'd say the room stood off,

gave room to the view, gave view to the mountain.
The roof-slope was made of window filled by sky,
such a cirrus of light which bulged and burned through glass
all the way from Uncanoonuc, today free of mist.

There was a bed in the room which seemed a mile wide
and we lay on the far side of its shore. There had been
the darkening that had given us the shock of rain
which when it ran its rivulets down the glass ran over us.

Then light poured back, and there was not only light
but air enhancing its warmth to heat. Be calm,
be calm, said Uncanoonuc, first I give you dark and rain
which makes you mysterious even to your own touch.

Then I give you light which inspects every crevice of room
and draws from you this squint, this shrinking away.
Be calm, it said, be examined and be seen at length,
and be seen at height, be seen at breadth, be seen at depth.

Arcimboldo's Bulldog

To a Sliver of Sicilian–American Sky

You water a bramble on the State House lawn.
A punch, you say, is often tenderer than a kiss,
politesse the broken, look-down-its nose vase
the day the green tea-makers run out of green tea.
An American highway's an alley choked with thorns,
you go in your pyjamas to breakfast at the café;
the bronze dog sheds its chains, and starts to growl.
The Men's Room kept for only men is as defunct
as indoor rain that drums upon a ten-foot leaf.

You're sure when the convention comes to town
and the lifts crowd with tattooed tattooists
it's only you and I know how complexity breaks

the skin as a claw, in scarlets, greens and blues.
Who are tattooists, you ask, *to speak of tattoos?*

The Woman Among the Nerudas

I hunger for your sleek laugh
Neruda

All the Nerudas muster, as if from nowhere,
like a flash-flood of doubles. There is not one of them
who feels he does not own that lugubrious smile.
Each draws around him like an overcoat the air
of *I am the Neruda*. Some great men, for security,
hire twenty men who look exactly like themselves.
Bonaparte's asylum-garden was crowded out
with loonies in bicorns and tails. A similar purpose
infuses the Nerudas: they blend and are safe.
This cloud of lookalikes seems to make it clear
that your uncommon, very un-Chilean voice
and umbrella which is firewalled and not grey
down with the grey umbrella of caps might be
the perfect Neruda, among the Nerudas, disguise.

What the Gulls Teach

This is the physical world, say the gulls, its reality is brusque,
its edges sharp and chaffing, its truths unnegotiable,
its gulls monsters of ego. They say the square and the air above it

is a vacuum sucking in gulls. They are drawn to its light,
how it shapes facades, has deep sides, and inclines all color
towards the intensity of white. They say this is the light that has

their heads duck beneath their wings as if they are reptilian,
when they retch to get more voice. Their masks, they say,
are lit as they peer out of dark at the swamp of light

down into which they circle and *yell, yell* – do not be fooled
by those that came before, those that come after. These are
gulls that were and never will be such unholy mob ...

Most distant, most near, do you not hear these cries
when they are so loud and when the show's for one night
and when the square could be ocean the other side of which

you strain to listen, close your eyes? Did you know that gulls
have been known to live for a hundred years,
that their ballyhoo dreams it is the rarest specimen

which extends twenty metres in each direction a leaf,
which separates out and opens over the square its petals,
which blooms in decibels, extends its many tongues?

Empath to the Punctured Kevlar Helmet

World is the head inside. The jump of the optic nerve.
Its Uzis are genteel. Its arbiters are deaf.
Add to it the lips that are less a grin than a grave.
Its guns hang like salamis. Though they are bereft
of protein they somehow often seem to bleed.
They're tagged with the tenderloins. The new Pietà
is now only hands with no body to be lowered.
World is the otiose oils. It is the stigmata.
I am the lopsided and the flagrant heart
pierced by all the needles the blowpipes blow.
World burns in my acids. It is too much fat,
too much glucose. I offer it a stomach that by now
can only manage honeydew and cantaloupe;
I offer it hunched self, hair-fall. My baby tooth.

Ugly World to Empath

Your spinal reflex, coddling at its base the warmest ever spot,
so tiny, says: withdraw. It feeds your despair
through the reed of the street-player's clarinet.
It is the mirror neuron, which looks at the war
and finds a war more terrible looking back.
It is gene and cloned cell. Whatever littlest grief
is a magnified self, which lowers, then cranes its neck.
Better, says the reflex, to feel nothing, if
every cell in you is someone else's yell.
If the oily chain seems to make it hesitant
the lift that heads down, heads up. It is full
of black flowers. The narrow streets of existence
are all tight corners and tall trucks.
They are both through-routes. And cul-de-sacs.

The Vanishment

'...if you might be the one who'll find her,
she wore a red brooch on her coat,
it was an oval of stones with one stone missing,
she had a gap between her teeth;
her teeth looked big because her hair was short,
she had squeezed her plump toes into shoes
which were at least a size too small

and as I let go, she let go of my hand,
and when I looked she was not there,
and counters were doors laid on their side
and where she'd been there was just the store
and the feet, the feet, so many feet
making the floor creak like voices which were
louder than any calling of my name

and the escalator, from the very top,
seemed to be empty of anyone at all
where it plunged between floors,
went down through a darkness and appeared again
and above the noise made the louder noise
of its chains going round and round,
clacking on, clacking on, on and on.'

For the Vanishing Twin

Born of the same gene, though she died in the womb,
I imagine her, mother, as if she had lived
so brittle of bone she was inclined to break
twice each bone you never broke once,
to suffer migraines, panics and swoons,
to whistle a note before she slept
and be seated, always, to the left of you,

and her whole demeanour, like yours,
be drawn to the gap between her teeth,
her trust of plainer clothes offset
by your love of turquoise, yellows and pinks.
Every cold you did not catch she caught.
If you spoke abundantly for two
she mimed to your words, hid in her hair,

as if disappearing she hid in her hair.
So robust, so calcium-rich, you fought
to keep her with you for ninety years
and to hold somehow inside your chosen name
the names she never had
which hung like strange chemises on the rail:
Esther, Emily, Emmeline.

Portrait in the Gaudi Mirror

As Gaudi had it, the curved line belongs to God
and in his house no force can straighten it.
The man and woman, lost in its spaces, give the nod
to the glass. The Gaudi house rolls
in its shackles around them. It is less house than wave
which buckles physics and seeing and seems to fill

itself with faces like these. Gingerly at first, they appear
and smile into the length of the mirror.
They are strange but as they rise they certainly peer,
followed by torso and feet. They stand side by side,
her hair scooped the wrong way by the glass.
Then she stands alone, in space she has to wade,

one foot foreshortened. When she perches on the chair,
he turns his back and looks up.
They re-link as if at an altar. They disappear.
They reappear. They disappear. They reappear. They seem
like a pleat in glass.
Old Arnolfini and his wife once posited a dream

of eternal wedding, tree at window, little dog.
That tree six hundred years later
has barged into the room and filled it with a fog
of blossom. It is his duck-tail, her hair tucked in her scarf,
you can just pick out in the mirror behind,
reflected tinily. This is their reliquary life.

Come, come, she says, tugging softly at his clothes,
we've manzanilla olives... Shcwick!
goes his camera and the sepals of the shutter close
to a peephole which as quickly springs back to rebuff
all but the entirety of his face.
And the little dog, lost through the atoms, *woofs*.

The Chorus of the Fathers
Addresses the Shuqualak Hermit

Give a cup of water, or die for someone.
Learn the minus-division, divide
a foolhardy thirteen into a fretful one.
Speak or do not speak of thirteen men

who answered to the six men trapped
in a crack of oxygen a thousand feet down,
which one end showed as much
of their boots as the other showed of their heads.

Of the thirteen men who went down
to save the six none came back up,
of the six trapped men, one crawled out.
In your solitude, your minus infinity,

you cannot do the mathematics of how
a life of instinct chooses to serve
the impossible decimal point of sacrifice.
A one hauls thirteen times its weight.

Divide thirteen into one. The outcome
is less than one and starts with a zero.
You are the water-halt, the point at which
the greater number is added or subtracted

and separates the living and the dead,
the zero into whom is divided
these thirteen, these million ghosts.
Water reaches your royal taps, and power

your bulbs though almost all of them
already have blown and only one burns
enough light for you to dream you hear above
the voices, the tap-tapping, in the pipes.

The Shuqualak Hermit Replies

'Of otherness I do not know how
to talk in a roomful of talkative mouths
among whom I sit without oars
when a circle rotates a rowboat

when it spins the sky spins another hour
of your life which spins another month
and when whisky drinks them the voices
rise up like a squall of fortitude

they will have to talk louder over
waves of music which also talk
I have been to the room before and felt
a sentence run from lips and be lost

I thought how complex is this organism
the most frightening in Creation
which can make a hundred calculations
while it raises a hand to its cheek

when it speaks, when it speaks pathways
so many to the same place all at once
sometimes eight of them hog a couch
and my friend the hermit who has lived

alone in a shack was terrified I could tell
by this state of being able to be seen
as if it was a thing that was not him at all
poor thing I think he thought he wished

to take it home again and let it rest
he said the people and the room and talk
were like a conference of bowling balls
in a bag that could not keep its shape'

Arcimboldo's Bulldog

The Quince Tree is Finally Flowering

They all agreed I was sick. The one who was not theirs
who knew bewilderment as a room with shelves.
Who knew the mother as the one who swapped
looks with the father, who entered his look.
They crossed at too steep an angle, like sky
that moved over too fast and brought with it clouds
that darkened a whole field and then spilt light
as if each change was a different day.

Should I run to the end of the garden
which seemed to grow narrow and go on and on
to where the father made an altar of my name
as if his voice, his gravity, was not a priest's,
as if after he had spoken I would grow?
When I tried to live inside this boiling sound
I felt the fit was perfect but that I could not be seen
and laid out stones to prove that I was there.

The quince tree was, was not, in the garden.
It was there in green shadow. Was it there in its pale flames?
When I dreamt of it, every hair of every leaf
spread a corona of alertness. But it was all green,
it was a lowliness of green. It was my life
without a blossom's blind utensils. I loved to fondle
the greenness of each leaf, soft in my fingers.
One night, the quince tree took me by surprise.

The Rain-Charm

'…the shaman returns with all kinds of things'
Ted Hughes, *Letter to Moelwyn Merchant*,
June 1990

Tall as a church, he was tall as a church
stooping over my crib. He stooped,
he leant, where his upper half could lurch
the rest of him into view and shift his weight
from one hand to the other. I saw the pulse
bulge in his wrist, bulge and race;
when he leant, when he stooped, his gaze
implied the prospect of grace;
then, as his torch yawed, of something else.

Upside down, it revealed how
he dwelt in his features. The straight,
possibly angry line of the mouth below
the philtrum's furrow, dark to one side,
the spider veins in his cheek.
When he looked over, his face filled with blood
and became less face than flesh-mask;
he'd suffused his clothes, it seemed, which shed
a peaty odour elevated to a reek.

There was ear-hair, there were sideburns
in need of pruning, leggy and overgrown.
There were eyebrows crosshatched like thorns
reaching but not meeting;
there was the stray, forehead jib
of hair which fell away, until he brushed it back.
The torch was dropped, picked up, then flooded
my face: '…I am Crag Jack's
grandson come to lift you from the crib.'

His old jacket seethed with microbes,
there was a patch on one elbow but not the other,
a briar-scratch on his earlobe;
his fingernails were chipped, as hard as horn,
there was moss in his socks;
his trousers were soaked to the waist, clung-to by seeds
of the meadow-grass he'd waded,
brushed by the laden reeds;
and, in his hair-roots, ticks.

It was Pastor Hughes come calling, I thought.
When the torch-beam skidded
and squirted up so he was caught
first at that angle, then this,
I shivered, sensed his pupils dilate:
…for a moment I thought it was my father.
That squelch, squelch as he walked
suggested he had crossed in waders
at the widest point of the river, now in spate.

When he sighed and spoke his voice
provoked, soothed, provoked and soothed:
there was intensity, there was excess
and both were carried forward in his sigh.
The shaggier, riper, overripe
vowels rolled around, the tongue
struck the back of the teeth;
the '*t*'s fell like gutter-drips among
whatever else was shuffled to his lip

when he read to me – while I slept –
what seemed like a lesson and my sleeping brain
caught what signal it could intercept.
It was like a growly recording, played
to me in sleep, in delta sleep,
a voice now fulsome, now terse
played to fingers which rapidly copied it.
'Dream', he said, 'the black verse
which shakes but cannot break your sleep.

See, I have deep pockets. Here's what I found in there
for you. This will be our secret.
My lush and pendulous voice will wear
through you a runnel, the drip,
drip of it on the sternum will cut a groove
deeper and deeper. Even when
you've no idea what you're saying
(and may simply whisper a soft *amen)*
your mouth will start to move

like a mouth at first miming then trying
to speak. At first you'll copy
every cadence and every dying
fall, I know. As if to bite the hand that fed
and cajoled and guided you,
at length you'll spurn the source. The lip-sync
will lose the lips. The time
will come when you'll think
it was you who said what I said.'

Arcimboldo's Bulldog

Fellini Beach

(1994)

The Water-Garden

The zoological squeaks of perambulators pass.
Down and round to the Water-garden go the long steps.
Chipped statues, on worn patches of the grass,
Hold utterly still the bird-bath that rescinds
An offer of water, shrunk to a stain in the heat.
Rigid Noah outstares the fountain's drops:
The bronze discolours, as the four embodied winds
Divide their separate powers about his feet.

The drops fly, bubble in deluge, and dissipate.
What is it, then, that eludes? Everything
Offers up the emblem of its shifting state.
Ephemeral the squabble of sparrows bathing;
The tree can grow no further inside its cramped cage;
The bubbles cling, or tremble, volatile.
A far roar pumps up a disconnected rage.
The empty pool implies the crocodile.

from *Fellini Beach* (1994)

A Spinster on the London Underground

My queasy boss leant over – halitosis:
If you could perhaps possibly if you wouldn't mind
Work a little late... I mimic his voice, softly.
A harsher protest sleeps where it cannot reach
The air. I stayed, cursor-tranced, sufficiently dull
But gracious – my last attempt to be beautiful.

And now I must confront my nightly torment
Of bodily nearness, the elevators, warm wind;
A veil between me and distasteful smells;
Chance knuckles brushing against my hand.
I must hunch myself more cautiously to ensure
My demeanor protects my body, which is pure.

Where there had been space, sufficient space,
A subterranean brief: '...maintain your own aura.
Don't have that gigantic stranger swaying
Over you like a tree, get through untouched,
Your concertina of credit-cards squashed flat
Against your nervous heart, where father sat.

Resist the canter, watch without watching –
When the stations' glare yields to darkness that
Plunges you into dull faltering light, eschew
Your doubled reflection through which a flight
Of underground cables comes close and flees
And makes a panic of light upon your knees.

Relinquish your arm-rests, without risking the elbows
Of the imbeciles which slouch either side.
Disregard the route-plan, the lighted signs
Or the appointment you made, nagged by
The sickly dread you would not make it. Be
Wary of all the evidence to the contrary:

Arcimboldo's Bulldog

However much you hope, or think, that it is,
The station you next stop at is not *Temple*.
The noises rise through the carriage-boards.
Hold your position exactly right. Down along
The platforms and tunnels a stifling wind blows.
Pick the bits from your skirt now. *Everyone knows.*'

'Do Poor Tom Some Charity'

Up in the dock, smiling-dumb
In waders and muddy overcoat –
Divertissement for the gallery's ennui –
Laughter muffled into comity –
Stood the Accused, placing on
The rail his broad hands as if about
To issue forth, but sitting down again.

                The queasy magistrate
Epilogised: 'Clearly there's
Not a precedent that I
In all my wigged murmuring years can equate
With this aberrant countryman's affairs.
Swallowing frogs, especially eight,
Is odd gluttony indeed, a *lusus naturae.*
The question's the extent to which the human gut's
A hostile environment
For a common frog.' (Chortles). *Order!* 'The point

Is, if we might, for a moment, extricate
Judgement from the gastric sediment,
Why to swallow?'

The Accused beckoned down his throat –
The moistening grim hollow
For the stricken victims, to acids sent,
A bellyful of insects in a sump of sour wine.
With imbecilic theatre, he drew back his coat,
Clasped
Something from its hook-hung lining and –
To the sound of the gallery's heavenward gasps –
Held it up wriggling, and swallowed…

Eight? *Nine.*

Calmly, the replaced hand:

A swathe of revulsion went round and the frog's legs beat.
The jury grew webbed feet.

from *Fellini Beach* (1994)

Cassiobury Lock

The stripped boys you watched plunge from the bridge
Into a lit oblong of canal, who disdained
The walls that rose too closely were a flash
Of incandescence, their skinny stomachs pumping
The shouts of an impetuousness beyond you.
Neither them nor the kingfisher today. Only
The eerie lock-gates which seem to tremble
Against winter water, loud drips clattering
From the drenched timbers, expressing the miles
Of dropped levels it took to find this level.

White into dark below, the bubbles wriggle, fizz:
Weeds in the mortices of the meeting shafts
Exploit a little soil, straining out of the dark
For what light there is, all winter's weight
Shuddering to drop from the upper level:
Diagnosed, struck by intermittent visions
Of the truth of it and of nothing better,
Already in the company of something else
You know, as well as I know, the pressure behind
Is made of volume and is made of depth.

Beneath us: sheer power, the strange slapping echoes
Of being enclosed by narrow walls which give
Order to shapeless water. *Think of me here.*
I come here often, for the air, humming and alone.
Stood beside you, father, sensing your weight of hands
Deep in your coat, I regard you now (I realise)
Almost as an old man, and hearing the weir roar
Am dismayed by the pathos of your frame
Above the weeping crossbeams of the gates below:
A reluctance to keep, a reluctance to shed.

from

Competing with the Piano Tuner

(1998)

Mirror Angled at Sky

'... In the morning the mirror is consulted again,'
said Doctor Johnson, but
not of this one dumped in the back of a Peugeot truck:

it is left, one corner broken off, among the riven architraves,
and won't be consulted again.
It is in with the ripped out sinks, the sofa springs' dying octaves,

it is with the builder's rubble that is valueless.
Now that its silver leaf is
peeling off, it is pond water with gleams beneath the surface.

There is a frogspawn of rust-spots. Black stipple on mercury.
There is a cloudiness
of depth and current, scratched by teeth beneath the glass

but bright enough for provincial eaves and firs to crane
over – for the first glimpse.
The mirror is put out. It will not be consulted again.

First, there is the misplacement – a veiled indoor convenience
must cope will all that light.
It reflects a worm's eye view of what will soon evaporate:

the passers-by with collars up for whom spring broke
too early, knock wet
turgid blossom onto it – equally misplaced where breeze-blocks sit,

as incongruous as the fractured seventy eight
of Beethoven's *Fifth*
dumped in the stingers – where nature and something else conflate.

Second, there's the passivity – the mirror tilted as it is
reflects every detail
of onrushing sky – the gulfs of blue and weightless cumulus

that drift like floes, that billow, fly, and break apart.
And so I think this bit
of junk's not just the still reflecting point of art

but may be likened to a certain juncture in
the history of clouds,
at which formations such as these might part to glimpse

maelstroms both human and equine, far below,
and which will yet
tear softly apart, to show the goings on of god knows what.

Lastly, there are the soft concealments – the mirror invokes
the droplets
of wet that steamed off with the last to smile in it:

the youthful nurse's theatre of unwitnessed face,
the couple who
moved in and out of it some twenty times a day.

Now all that consults it is sky. Soon, it will go
to the council dump,
but here finds cloud after cloud moving slow

though its skin of liver-spots is utterly still,
and under the glass pours this
bright moving floor or conveyor belt, freckle-faced.

Arcimboldo's Bulldog

Ways of Seeing with Heatstroke

I'll start again. A horse that is led on a rein
down an alley that is narrow, by a girl.

A hand, a rein, a rein that is drawn
by a hand down an alley, plus a horse.

A horse that is walking down an alley
that is narrow has a girl, attached to it.

A rein that loops gently, down an alley,
with a horse and a girl at either end.

A ring at the centre that holds the rein,
holds the girl, holds the horse. It is silver.

The blossom that floats, that is sucked
down the alley, that is blown from its branch,

that is a draught of rain, of ochre snow.
The sun that bulges into the alley

or the alley that cramps the sun, mostly dark.
The ground that clops upon the hooves.

from *Competing with the Piano Tuner* (1998)

Lines to an Unemployed Actor

And in some metropolitan station,
among MacNeice's cans and the roistering files
of steam, the pinched soul fidgets for elbow-room.
The steam's from the Kitchen of Sideswipes,
Chang Tsai's laundry where only you speak Chinese,
the vents of the Merlin club, the burger bar's sinks.
After RADA and its clarity of reception
and the taking of *Midsummer Night's Dream* to Japan
comes the interference, tuning itself in.
You're right. Those vents emit a Faustian steam.

Any long distance telescope will teach you how
many thousands of years go by between
the star's birth and its picture hovering in.
So famished by now for Polonius, or Aguecheek,
or perhaps a little murky Bosola,
you cycle sixty miles a day around The Square Mile
delivering parcels, steer a panicking pony-tail.
You are getting fitter and fitter, you tell me,
threading more than taxis each time you pedal
from Cheapside to Threadneedle Street.

Your dying aunt left you a barometer, you say,
with which to read the atmospheric pressure.
Far from home, in the hundredth city of ingratitude,
so it is you're offered your first speaking part
(with lines that are a doddle to extemporize)
but due to unforeseen technical difficulties
and the overactive libido of a hack composer
the soundtrack is much too loud for the film.
Now comes the tricky bit: superimposing your voice
upon the movements of your own mouth.

Lapwing, Lark, Linnet...

Remember your eggs, brother, fragile under glass?
At one end the murky Grebe beginning the descent
to the truly tiny from the huge, whose yolks
succumbed to your pin and bicycle pump?

Remember your revered collection, up in the loft
like a light left on, burning all that electricity?
Once, you could feel its smoothnesses when your fingertips
were still a centimetre from the shells.

Now I'm told, this morning, the oafish roofers
(one jigging in his earpods, three idle to respond)
have pitched the slates through the glass and crunched
the shells to a cataclysm of broken bits.

The bits stuck to their soles, like stones to tyres,
they spread them about and did not know they did
for which act, I'm told, you'll get compensation.
The world laps at your feet and you do not budge.

Linnet, Magpie, Ouzel... Like sunlight sieving
through the slates the fragments of sky blue, white,
litter the loft roll. Once, this would have been
the work of hobnails in a frowsty Eden.

Each day I hope in vain for the letter
which says: '...they have broken my eggs.
They have broken my eggs. They have broken my eggs.'
You say: *the roof no longer lets water.*

Chinese Fish

The voiceover's spiel is either educating or
Appeasing those who wait for takeaway food;
Tired of playing to indifference, the set is on the blink:
From the tissue of the Madagascar Periwinkle,
Says the voice, *a genetically identical version*
Of the original is cloned... Competing with
The contraflow of steaming bags and soiled sterling
That traffics an Oriental tailback of smells
Computer graphics show dividing cells.

Illuminated in their brilliant hues below
The Chinese fish mouth behind their lurid screen:
As if lit up for the bored night class, plugged in,
Two nibbling the eerie mirror of each other or
Dancing to the commentator's mincing tune,
As if poised, for mutual cannibalism, or
Scoring the arcs of their own bisection –
Identical, inflated, spared their own weight –
Appear to kiss like cells, and separate.

Burning

Apples coming back, the firs, the dog-roses wagging
in the firelight or clamouring like goodbye, as if *curious*.
It is dark, and we are stinking up next door's smalls

left out on the washing line, among the moist petals.
We are burning what will spare the removal van's springs
when in a few days we leave this chaotic house at last.

Fire. Flames leap close and drive us off, woo us back – they crawl
the surface of some warping thing, or bubble up
from under, steam through a crack, break out into glorious flower.

My lengthening boy lounges in the spattered chair
shortly we'll chuck on fire like a holy throne, and see roar –
his pupils the pinpoints of an ancient seriousness,

he flares out of the dark, from trainer to red shirt to cheek,
if one cheek is dark, one burns. Away with it all –
poke, play with, stare fascinated. And so he does, half bored.

It is no good at all to be so outnumbered by
belongings, as if marooned in a warehouse, without exit.
So we burn as much as we can, watch it collapse or put out a limb

of supplication – a charcoal spirit surrendering,
burned away from its iron, from its black lock.
Goodbye, then, to clutter and the house that tolerated it.

Let our varnish hiss and explode, blister and cackle
long into the night and send fireflies up
beneath the turgid apples, dog-roses, the attentive firs.

Beyond its racket there is such stillness, a dog's bark,
the sound of children going to bed. We are alive, for sure,
and world is everywhere, our feet now more able to walk us.

from *Competing with the Piano Tuner* (1998)   39

The Tower of Pisa and the Mudflat Horses

When one team of men tried to stop the tower from falling
another team was trying to drag the horses from the mud.
The mares that had strayed from their grazing
into the bogs fought until they could fight no more,
though talked-to and encouraged in their ebbing strength
they sank up to their necks, they jerked back their eyes
and trod themselves deeper as panic gripped
then relinquished them, helpless as eroded stone.
The Tower of Pisa, seven hundred years old, as if
organically alive and helpless in its clay,
shifting in one night as much as it does in a year
had creaked south like the next stage of an old intention.

The tonnage of lead weights on the north side
holding the tower at its angle acted as a winch
to the stricken animals, as if steadying them,
the weight of horses added to the weight of lead.
The liquid nitrogen pumped into the foundations
to freeze the failing clay also froze the clay
beneath the horses, and gave them a floor
as if the tower's roots reached as far from it as them.
When their legs strove like pistons the horses felt
the whole tower draw at their breast like a harness.
All they and the engineers of Pisa could do
was slow down for a further hundred years or so
the next few degrees of the downward arc
of its thirty second fall through eternity. All
the men could do was save the horses so they might
pick a path between bogs and find supportive earth
for perhaps, God willing, a centimetre of the arc.

Human endeavour was everywhere. Much stayed as it was.
Both rescue teams raced against an incoming tide.
The tower had to stick fast in the mud
and the horses stumble up out of it
weakly as foals, one stay and the other move,
and grinning men declare an amnesty with clay,
and the world resume its balance and its shape,
and horses stand straight so a tower could lean.

from

To the God of Rain

(2003)

A Futurist Looks at a Dog

I do not see godmother's adoring pet
as you do, nor know him by name; neither can
I keep the present he keeps:
his six little steps to match godmother's one.

I see instead every stride the dog has made
in the last twenty metres at once,
the sum of strides per second jumbled up
on top of one another – its tail

a cactus of wags, its rapid legs
a sort of tailback of centipedes,
a strobile of stunted steps, a carwash brush,
two bleary propellers rotating.

Above it, the leash in flight is many leashes
whipping and overlapping,
a flung silver net, a soundwave,
each stride a new species of leash;

the dachshund once set in motion
embarks upon another existence,
and godmother's pet as you know him
vanished twenty, no, thirty strides back.

from *To the God of Rain* (2003)

Laws of Probability

So your feisty stepmother and my therapist,
one October, though we did not know it, got to mount
the same ornate elephant in the extreme North

of Uttar Pradesh – seven thousand miles from home –
with as much exquisite apathy as if they shared
the Tube from Baker Street to Euston Square.

They shrieked, we may presume, and held onto their hats
that far east of the great Syrian desert,
and did not for a seasick moment suspect how close

to you and I they came, sat back to back,
– quanta of heat trembling in the spaces.
To me it seems as likely they should meet

as the two of them should conspire to find
the one mosquito in Goa with a ring on its back leg.
So picture them, their shoulder-blades touching,

oblivious for a while to their respective flocks
of deferred or inherited children,
flung out on the long stopping curve and jostling up

between the loose petals of their blouses
a pocket of warm and inconsequential air,
a new species of commonplace.

Distiller's Unstable Daughter Explains her Absence from the Class

The men have come out of the ground again.
I have to tell you the successful distiller
of spirits has a seventh tall daughter.

Listen. They call me from under the street.
They lean on shovels, down under the awning
in the hole in the pavement, exposing the bright wires.

They wear hard-hats, and though not magicians
will restore to me my visibility –
green eye, cheek, gangling leg, painted toe-nail.

Yes, they ease me back into view. And I, slipping
in and out of my most perfect of minds –
monster of my yellow psychiatrist – step down

into the sunlight. The sex is clean and necessary.
The orange awning, warmed from the inside, contains
the closest approximation of day.

Now that I can be seen, I am lethal. See –
my *vividness*. But will my six sisters and mother
and distillery-owning father deep into their storm

have the eyes, the twenty/twenty vision
against the old glaucoma, the eclipsed pupil?
Now there's a question for the blind optometrist.

The Deaf School

Not the Institute, but the place the deaf girl took me to,
obeying as it did
roughly the same laws of perspective:

bare of indulgence, of sound, of bloom,
the end of the line
for the scaffolder's blunder, horn, the playground's scream.

Bare walls – an odd foreshortening –
and a sense
of hieroglyphics hidden, so to speak, in moving currents

like the light that lapped and flowed from end to end
as the blind knocked,
as the pencil rolled, without soundtrack.

Strange all my attempts to reach the deaf woman should
imply she had
something I did not. Sat opposite her, I'll not deny

I saw myself reflected, as if wholly visible,
deprived
by her deafness of language, unable to speak.

I was disturbed by her focus – by those rapid pupils
brought
to finger-exercises, sans violin, sans bow:

and I sensed the voiceless boom absorbed by her skin,
her nerve-ends;
I sensed her feel but not hear my indefinite noise.

Though our patient interpreter broke brilliant crumbs
between us, I knew
in the blind's gusts of light pale Karen was both

prospect of water and of sighted island,
and I
the churning ferry, its clapperless bell.

from *To the God of Rain* (2003)

To The God of Rain

i.m. Gregor Fisk (1973-1997)
who suffered from Cerebral Palsy

A dry tap, Father, I was a dry tap
Expecting the news of water –

At birth, the savage coulters
Of my mother's pelvis drawn

Through my brain's clay left it
Rutted and squeezed out of shape,

Lord, baffled like raw soil;
Nothing grew in it, and you

Knew better than I what would
Be my salvaged crop.

There was this bit of scrap,
The sliced sod. This glossy furrow.

There was this space. Forgive me,
I'd always thought you'd teach me,

Lord, how to be wise,
But my thoughts were like moths

Thumping in the webs;
There was this space on my brow.

How could this shapeless big body,
This slowness to follow

And inner wilderness in need
Of water be squeezed

Arcimboldo's Bulldog

Through the narrow eye,
Lord, of the citadel's needle?

There was this space. This space.
There was this space on my brow

Which awaited the licks of your rain.

The Wasps' Nest

'The hole through which everything poured, beneath
    the rug …'
wrote Liu Hsün, but we had a wasps' nest.
Almost as if our great room of desk and clock
    and wing-chair had begun to sag

and sink, where some keep cash, we had a wasps'
    nest. And board after board
blocked the view. So did the rug.
Beneath castors and claw-feet – though its
    towers and ladders were crude –

it began to draw at the whole house, bowed the long
    joist beneath us
like the weight of the afterlife.
It toiled in its place like an engine softly burning gas

on the wick of itself, dipped deep. And this was
    strange. We feared
the flame of it. Not that
it seemed to threaten us but the heads we heard gently
    butting the boards

that traversed the pit far below, made us afraid. We
    feared the swarm.
It was our thoughts though,
not Council steam, went down beneath the floor
    of the towering room

and the water lilies of the Chinese rug floated in light
into the furnace of stumbling wasps
to sense something that might make us welcome at a
    later date

burning out a gulf through the cracks and knot-holes,
 beneath the lid.
At times, it seemed innocuous,
a glue pot, a piecrust slapped on pocked timbers, a
 pat of swallow mud,

but at others, forgive me, we grew uncertain if the
 nest was glued to the house
or the house was glued to the nest.
At such times, it seemed the house was perched above
 a precipice

as if all its roots and foundations were suddenly flying
 out over it,
just hanging there, while
the wind of twenty thousand wings beneath it took
 its whole weight.

It was a summer of drought, and I stepped into the
 rug's radiance where
the great bay printed its shape
and I sensed the nest massage the soles of my bare
 feet like a jacuzzi of fire

and we wondered if perhaps it was a symbol of wealth
 sent to us,
or of bankruptcy, or both? There below
was it the windfall, or the bailiff's notice slapped on
 the dusty window?

Or was it a gateway? Again and again we dreamed
 the multitudes
of wasps, each one
among the many like a fizz in a helmet or an
 armourplated ohm

crumbling the breach, until the din filled our heads,
    rose above tape-hiss
and kettle, Mozart and the mains.
And we traced the vaguer image of ourselves in
    earphones

in the lens of the television once we had switched it
    off, seated as if
at one with the room's
curvaceous perspectives, in caps, unable to drown out
    the hum.

Was it some sort of centre, beneath our feet? It seemed
    to coincide
exactly with the balancing stem
of the rug's huge floppy lily. It seemed almost as if the
    stem led

further down into the heart of things, as if such solace
    depended
on such combustion,
perhaps, or as if somehow such depths of turbulence
    were required

to hold the petals so, stock still. The pit of crawling
    coals,
we dreamed, seemed to draw in
everything to itself like a cistern that fills and fills
    and fills

and melts the wax walls of its sides like smelting
    gold and dissolves
our shape and overflows
though the Chinese lily does not for a moment
    tremble. Nor change its pose.

Whisky Drinker Considers his Skirmish with Death

With so much hard ground rising to meet me I should be glad of a
                                                          little sea.
What is heavier? Body or earth?
When they smack into each other they are of equal weight.
We do each other damage.
                    The mangled cockpit, the churned up bank.

The windscreen spattered, as if muck snowed. This much I recall.
I was upside down
in the ditch, and a sky
of tussocks and puddles and hooves thundering upside down
tilted at my chin
and Wagner still boomed at the speakers, a wheel ticked to a standstill.

... *running water,* I thought, that is the sound of running water.

This much I recall, but what of the moment of rolling,
like being inside the drum of a washing machine,
those seconds, those milliseconds which I cannot ever reenter,
when something *gasped* in mid air somewhat as if
it was the first leap
into the midwife's impersonal gloves, the drop over the edge:

all I *know* is, as I rolled, a rain of loose change fell to the ceiling
and my leaflets flapped and fluttered around me
like panicking birds trying to get the right way up.

                    A soft regurgitation of Glenmorangie.
Then light, the bright light, of heaven?

                    The policeman's lamp in the lane.
                              I heard his umbrella unwrap, like wings.

Not yet, Mr Death, am I your punctured minion
                              or your blue-eyed boy.

from *To the God of Rain* (2003)   55

In Italy (by Match-Light)

*'And I saw what looked like an angel, holding
in his hand the key to the Abyss ...'*

                                    Revelation 20:1

Once more he'll get the blob of sulphur to burst
alight, cupped so it will burn up:
see what you can, while you can. See, in

the sudden match's yellow-blue explosion,
your father's features – intent pupils,
nose-bridge, khaki collar and, in each pupil, *flame*.

Because the – *fucking* – kerosene lamp withholds
its merry wick he must read
by the light of matches your mother's insect-scrawl:

see the army tent's sail full of sulphur
sailing him, sailing him
ever further south – flapping and drumming.

On the crease of his brow a mosquito,
a moth's gigantic shadow purring across the page.
And this the last match. Be assured

he'll burn thumb and forefinger, pinched nails,
before he lets the last go out,
so bright. See how the charred stalk dips

against the entrusted dark, the match-wood hissing
to nose fluid forward, yielding to flame.
A while longer light. A while longer.

Every thought of him – like the orange nimbus
itself, or warplans he serves without understanding –
drawn to the sulphur's tear

like insects off the river.

Arcimboldo's Bulldog

from

The Blood Choir

(2006)

For the Seven Hundred and Forty Ninth Species
of Barbed Wire

Only the rain can cling to it, snatched away
by a rumour of air thickening then passing.
Let a hand try the same, we're told, and a trap

of razors will spring and close, spring and close.
(In it, they say, the body of a jackdaw left its feet
thirty metres from its head, which nonetheless

turned to address them: '... only half of us can make it
over the wire, half in the world, half out,
though the pale gas of morning rises on either side.')

Think of it: a contraption of blades coiled
along the top of the towering fence erected between
six hundred young men and their birthright.

One side of it thrive all the indices
of hunger, the other the many sorts of worldly apple.

from *The Blood Choir* (2006)

Spaniels in a Field of Kale

The two spaniels leaping and flying
like shadow and leaper, like leaper and shadow
sent in wider and wider circles,
the more they leap about, and chase
each other through the mile-wide depths of choppy kale,
the more they might be mistaken for
an upblown leaf, a lifted edge that balances
its catchment of light briefly like their coats
parting to the skin in the wind's combs
which cross the heath like a search-party, extending
the eerie coastline of the prison fence.
The logic of them, flopping and collapsing, flies
out in a northerly direction towards the last outcrops
of Scapa Flow, or keeps going with the rafts
of overushing altocumulus due west
to the land floes of Inishbofin, east to Orford Ness
or south to the lip of the Lizard, where it hovers panting
over the odd ellipsis of Land's End:
this before it takes the whole flight on rewind,
tracing it phase by phase until the dogs
refind the channel they have trodden flat
in the blowing field where the kale
springs up again in front of them, untrampled.
The logic of their leaping takes
the flight again, and then again, as if each flight
is the exercise without which its belly
would drag too closely to the ground,
and those tresses in earthbound flight
be a slip-leash, a sort of flowing yoke built around
the features of a little prune face,
a mouthful of yappy snarls.

The Blood Choir

After Goya

Consider how a young man sheds his name
and number, his boot-blister and tattoo,

his lisp, his wrist-scar and dental history;
how he sheds, in short, all that could not

be anyone's but his, the ancient encryption
of his fingerprint, the mole on the ball of his foot.

It is a terrible thing to witness the speed with which
he and twenty other inmates are drawn up,

stumbling backwards, into one another; how they grow
eerily identical webbed feet, webbed fingers,

webbed ears, and melt their bone-marrow down
to the kind of red glue that welds them together

at the pelvis, the abdomen and the chest
as if, well, some slow-moving animal penned

by a single rope, tugging at each wrist; some rhythm
of oars rowed, without a drum; some engine

which drives a sort of spirit replica straight through
the savage razors of the wire without a scratch.

2

The one, usually the strongest, the one
with the large X smeared on his forehead

invisibly in red, there for good however much
he tries to wash it off, the one who stands

above the rest at six foot three, the broadest,
most bullish-loud, who changes shape,

and always wears, like all the rest,
the identical bottle-green shirt, green trousers,

standard issue boots, mandatory snarl,
who changes shape in mind and in physique,

estranged self, say, into sea-inhabiting being,
willing ear into something with eight, no, fourteen arms,

something that leans its body weight forward
with no control of either limb or energy

but scrambles a disk of prison numbers,
carrying under each of its fourteen arms the head

of another grinning boy who carries
under each of his fourteen arms another grinning head.

3

The flash-point at the centre is red, red
as the sleep of reason. Note how

quickly the fluid in the ball-joints welds
hip-girdle to hip-girdle, their finger-bones thread

each other's rings, arms each other's sleeves;
how they seem to stand at roughly the same height

Arcimboldo's Bulldog

and swing their knuckles to roughly the same depth
as if hinged upon the same fine shank:

note how, when it shouts, there are twenty mouths
drawing on one capacity to breathe;

how its outer stockade is comprised
of every slightest elbow-movement that was made

in the last thirty seconds, seen all at once,
as if its dead weight were evolving the lightness

of a gossamer wing-beat, lifting it off the ground.
A warm wind blows all around it, blowing

hair in towards the centre. It bellows, dies,
looks down, drums the rubber of its many feet.

4

How can it be said to have any shape at all,
lacking love, asks the prison chaplain? Look how

it assembles, in its war-paint of tattoos:
long-necked and flatfooted, distorted as though

by a fairground mirror, growing hard pads
exactly where it needs them, developing

all that upper muscle, plates beneath the skin
and helmets so ridged they seem more like

mouldings of bone beneath the shaven scalp;
and pale, well yes, pale from a diet of dross

and having grown so long and awkwardly
in the dark, but strong, for having spurned love

as so much squandered oxygen, a Grimm's
fairy tale for the snug, a myth

not sticking to it – see how it stands, equipped
with the perfect armour of scorn, plus

steel elbows and steel knuckles, perfect
for the world it must enter and smash to bits.

5

Like something dying back, withdrawing once it has
gone out perhaps as far as it can go,

now dying back. Having flourished red,
having pitched into wilderness, the more its shouts

were wrung to liquid, the more it colonized space;
now dying back. See how the body of it

yields at the centre, and disassembles; how it first
drummed up its dream of sovereignty and now

gives it up, quietly; how it breaks apart, leaving
one boy to smile among his freckles

like the patron saint of shrinking violets,
another to rub his neck, one to blow his nose

and one to sigh, others to turn away, as if surprised
by daylight after the matinee, flung clear...

This is how the organism (having pulled and tossed
in its chains) detaches its many body parts

and disperses them towards some sort of roll-call:
Allam, Dunwoody, Cuedjoe, Burke,

Loy's Return

To be on your back, says Loy, mashed, while the stuccoed
saloon bar lurches up and dreams it floats
or dips into the wave, and the room goes bending and rolling;

to be nose-up in one boot, while the barmaid calls to you
for some unknown reason in French, *fucking* French.
Nu, this; *Vu* that. *Bonwee* or *Bonwat,* or something

like that. To claw your way up from the floor of the gents
by the taps, says Loy, setting off the hand-drier
to which you mouth a greeting, then drop back,

and having learned how tricky swimming is
after seven years and three months, a week,
a day, three hours inside, he says, to wake to find yourself

staring up from under water and holding your breath
until there's not a bubble to tell anyone you're there,
not a *fucking* bubble, if you'll pardon the French.

from *The Blood Choir* (2006)

The Ailing

Strange how the dropped crockery does not break
nor reach the floor, and no one notices. Here in this place
of locked cells and of lines kept reassuringly straight

things grow comfortable very slowly. The thought
swims in water brought to the boil, the huge and nameless event
steps in through the wall, and no one notices.

The click of the guard's shoe cannot quite catch up with
its metal tip. What might be a film plays in silence.....
And rueful Wilbur's sentence? Oh, a thousand years, served

in hair-fall and scissor-snips, if snip could catch the scissors
and he could remember how to play. Look how his arms
are secured behind his back, and hands slightly more

eager than his own have been fed through his sleeves
to yawn the bow softly across his cello.
Somewhere, years back, the first note snivels.

Arcimboldo's Bulldog

The Language School

The charges might as well be read out
in Chinese, Bantu or Dravidian

or not be read at all – they drift, they loop
like light that cannot turn a corner

or soundwaves that bend in and out
of some fidelity to the original. To whom

do they cling? Another dumbstruck boy
who does not speak the English they speak

or even hear it – all nape and haircut, sat
folded up in a Jesuit clasp

with hands in his armpits, perusing
with a sort of thick-lipped composure

the platypus-nose of his left trainer, as if it had
evolved out of kilter with the rest.

2

No is the blank, the zero, the lumpy zilch,
the bijou fuck-all the question solicits

and wishes-for: the litany, the plural of no.
It is the answer the question anticipates

before asking itself, surrounding no.
Do you have anything to say in your own defence?

The hiatus, the answer-in-minus scans
the many milliseconds of a second

that hang like a threat, scaring it
way up into the corner of articulation

where it ceases to exist.
Without fuss, or noise, or anything,

without changing expression or looking up
the only yes there is nods to a no.

The Echoists

They began by repeating all my words.
Now don't do that, please; *now don't do that, pleeeese …*
Whatever I tried to teach them, it was sent back
on its privileged plate untouched.

Before long, each statement and its echo became
one utterance. Whatever I said set off
their high-pitched and ironic echolalia
struck in the key of an old man's falsetto croaks

as if to say that anything I might choose to say
was in dire need of counterpoise. I, I; *I, I …*
I mean to say, I mean …; *I mean to say, I meeean…*
The echo got glued to every word, got stuck

like the man who went on hiccoughing for twenty years
and still hasn't quit. Long after I left them
behind razor wire, tall gates and bars the echoists
like tones in the wilderness, like semitones,

continue supplying on one frequency the echo
to the word. The echo clings to my explodents
and my glottal-stops, as it will for ten,
for twenty years, for the rest of my life.

The echo continues to spasm among
the dipped-in-light roots of my vocal chords,
a sort of eerie and distorting in-built heckle
forever speaking at the edges of its own sound

and weighing every word for its ingredient truth
as if to remind us language only ever belongs
to its blind creators, and the lake we drink at is full
of water and undrinkable water.

A Shithouse Reverie

I have often been afraid, but these early morning yells
exchanged like ritual blows set every single hair of me
on end, a spider of hair treading my nape, fear

staring from every hair – flung, into the early air,
from cell-window to cell-window like blades winnowing
and sharpening each other half way across (...while I

prepared myself in the toilet best as I could) the yells
called to the stifled yell in me suggesting I get
the whole of my body out double quick; they pushed back the bones

in my face through realignment after realignment
to where, at four years old, I stumbled into the fetch
of the wave that sucked me down beyond my father's reach

and held me under with open eyes, while my hair swarmed
all around me like an electric shock, and I looked
into the mirror of water that would not look back.

Shoe Gazing

McStein has a facial scar and mannerly sense,
Sol, so loud, in a perpetual lather;
Hodgkins's sly, intelligent, furtive way
the counterpoint to Bradley's manic brain;
Aziz, his inoffensive glissando of laugh;
Randals, infallibly drawn to the weak –

One by one, I dream them, whose crimes
rattle and bump behind them like a cortège of tin cans.
Their faces – I don't know how to say this –
are turning into mine. That smile.
It started and now it cannot stop.
A potential is mirrored like a shadow. It falls, like rain,

in the spaces between assumptions
and threads the body's interstices, goes into your bones.
Look. They have found my new shoes
and squabble, trying to read the label.
Into their white-as-sea-foam trainers,
earned for good behaviour, I slip an overcautious foot.

Why Dunwoody Smashed Every Pane
of the Stained Glass Window

Dunwoody doesn't know,
so how could I, or anyone?

Maybe because it was dark, from outside,
and its chained indoor rainbow

shut in from him by a giant lock
and that there's something in Dunwoody

which doesn't love a lock – perhaps –
something in him, or me, or we?

Is it him, or me, would like to think
of the churchwarden's silts of anger

stirred into clouds?
Or who'd find the saints false, on breaking in,

and though ending up with dark bottle-bits
prefer the thought, the both of us,

of bright smithereens, a hail of razors
and stalactites, a shattering of stars?

At Dusk, You Can Hear the Men Calling

The voices calling from cell windows
are like those held in the answerphone,
they fill the house, hopeful someone might speak back
but meet instead the infinite scope

for confession, hope, evasion and doubt,
self-entanglement, scorn − a crack
in the reinforced wall of silence.
At dusk the voices are almost eerie,

like the sound of drowning men far out at sea.
They fill the whole empty house
of the air and the trees and the heathland, aimed
with light's last dregs and onset of cold

at someone who is or is not listening either
on the next block or in the next world.

from *The Blood Choir* (2006)

Ground Bass

*Having confessed to the killing of some fifty five people, though adjudged legally
sane, created – it has been said – by the excesses of Soviet famine and deprivation,
Chikatilo was taken to the Serbsky Institute in Moscow for psychiatric evaluation...*
New York Times, *October 1992*

Don't talk to me of the soul; that after all
is the business of saints. Do you imagine it squats
on the shelf, thick with the beautiful references?

I think it moves the left half of the brain which moves
the right, etcetera. Through your two-way glass,
gentlemen, I was the wrong way around,

and though the left half of the brain is held responsible
for the actions of the right half of the body
I was confused as to what was left,

what right, what normally sloped one way
sloping the other. That mouth. Oh, I note your eyes
slip away in one movement and look down

as you throw a leg across the other, and sigh,
and brush your sleeves... windblown
and still recovering from the eleven flights

which lead you down, not up, and place
such a strain upon the muscles of the calf...
better, though, perhaps than that

secateurs of a lift (I see you smile)
which brings you down, down through the centre
of this old building by the light

Arcimboldo's Bulldog

of a flickering forty watt bulb which still
somehow refuses to blow.
                              I cause, I know,
your keyboards to click more avidly of late,

tracking white with bright ideas or shunting
the carriages which jostle and bump
and stall behind the cursor's engine

towards the slow ascent and descent
of understanding. I am the stump in mist
even your rainswell cannot dislodge

when everything floods like the yellow Grushevska
roaring at such a speed it swept away
and then washed up the evidence;

what I had sent out was brought back,
brought back, and ducked me towards
the final enfilade of flash-cubes in the snow:

Chikatilo the frozen. Prize of the Public
Prosecutor's Office. They say I have two souls.
One plausible tenth, they say, Andrei Romanovich

shows us by the light of day
while the other nine are out of sight…
You must forgive me. Your appetite of course

is one that has no bottom at all,
as if with each fresh morsel, full of protein,
the stone in the belly is appeased

but never fully satisfied, being stonelike.
Little Lena Zakotnova, Larisa Tkachenko,
bewildered Lyuba Biryuk in her thirteenth year,

Ivan Beletski picking apricots in sunlight
and the other fifty-one who strolled too close
to the centre, who rolled over one by one

in their skeins of drenched hair,
cling to my belt-buckle, cuffs, my fingertips.
The mortician's label is attached to their toes.

Should I continue? I think there is
something of the prurient priest at large
in your questioning, offended by what

most attracts and is enough to drop
your young assistant's elbow on the zero-key
of the machine which trundled in his lap

but now sends out (though he doesn't know it)
a flat line of zeros across the screen
beyond the last recorded intelligence

while he sips at his mug with startled eyes:
how is he to know, when the succession of noughts
suddenly jumps onto its second line

and then a third and then a fourth and fifth,
language has failed, and a new sort of wilderness
is being created as it is discovered

a centimetre at a time, offering no
distinguishing features or signs of life,
just more, just more and more of the same?

I give you what you most seem to want;
I give you what I give you.
                              The lift goes down.
I grew, that is to say, I grew there

Arcimboldo's Bulldog

in growth-spurts of infinite slowness
far from the dangerous surface:
beneath the upper light my glacial will

was legumes of stretched rock, so long
and tapering, like organ pipes sipping frozen water,
and the mile of my small intestine

wound down, down, in rock-folds
smooth as marble or polished obsidian
towards the crystal cave of the duodenum

thick with a white profusion
of snow-flowers along to the holly-like nibs of which
a gathering plump drip rolled

its undiluted acid – and froze:
the unusually developed (… it is said)
cerebellum bloomed in an overhead drapery

of frozen folia, shedding a fine frost…
Your lamps shine into me. I am
the spectacular efflorescence

of your spirit's ennui. Note how
your voices drop in my company
like Sunday hats removed in reverence, how

the fishmonger treasures my till receipt
and others my clippings, a single hair, a relic,
any faintest, obscurest relic of me

while the crowds trail past my door
as if my rarity were the wonder
and a certain sort of status conferred

by touching it, even by drawing close.
You greet me, shall we say, somewhere between
curiosity and fear – disturbed and intrigued

by a man with knowledge of the depths.
I grew too slowly,
                        while everything sped.
When the world developed requirements

it could neither articulate nor meet
I knew I had grown out of want
and I knew I had grown slowly enough

to do the dirty work, to wring the surplus
of moisture from Christ's sponge
though your hands, shall we say, were clean... it must

be fine to sit in your self-angelising
seat, clean-cuffed and manicured, confident your hands
will never be grubbied, shuffling papers...

When I lift my left foot in its chains
a tram stalls in rainy Rostov, then starts again.
Shortly, gentlemen, you'll squeal your chair-legs

and depart, gathering up your effects
and rewinding your machine, leaving me
to the very last of my several attempts

to prolong the conversation... words dissolving
with my latest expression, fade by fade,
though held in your magnetic signal

like the voice from the other side, to be
played over and over for the clue.
Tape me a moment longer, though your eyes betray

Arcimboldo's Bulldog

involvement inflected with unease,
a weariness laced with tact...
What of the age, I ask you, which demands a beast

more slyly itself, more extravagant,
to manage needs so complex?
I felt my acts drawn larger, as if a pantograph

first set down the point that followed
every crevice and outline of each act
while the second point, as if instructed,

enlarged it perhaps some twenty times:
and the arms that linked the two pistoned back
and plunged like mechanical elbows

on their swivelling rivets; so both continued
moving as one, faithful to every detail
the first discovered at the tip of its point

and the second merely reproduced,
until the gadget completed the outline both
of the act and its intricate implications

the more you looked, as if you looked through
the atoms at exploded atoms beneath
and saw some terrible truth there.

Sometimes I dreamt it was God.
Or perhaps a minor, unassuming god
sometimes inclined to whisper a little

of the flame that could burn a halo
out of these zero temperatures
– now orange, now yellow, now blue –

or flare up, of a sudden, like caught gas
and burn away my stained cape,
and burn away my hands, and burn away my feet,

and burn away my body out of which
a body might grow, warmed on one side
to a sort of rosy flush by the flame

that infuses crystal with creeping colour
and bursts from the frozen heart itself
and fills my mouth.

from

Priest Skear

(2010)

Riding the Ghostly Velocipede

It's said that drowning can be beautiful
(...though the ones who said it were not the ones who had to drown).
The surrender, perhaps, to the arms of water

Shelley was gripped by – able to fly, but not to swim.
And this my bid to join the fellowship of the drowned –
more terrible than beautiful – these the fathoms striped

with a route-map of light, this my bicycling down and down
on the pedals of my feet with my arms thrown out wide
as if to steer through imploding water the velocipede

whose handlebars I tried to grip, but could not catch.
I was four, father, and washed too far from your reach
and I somersaulted several times with weed, with weed

around my neck, my feet, until you flashed me back to the light;
until you fished me out like a pup from the drowning bucket.

from *Priest Skear* (2010)

The Interment

When you saved me, father, saved me from drowning
though the Atlantic that tried to drown me called me back
I spent an hour burning my shoulders to bury you in sand

from your chin to your toes, while you lay like a dead man
snoozing with crazy hair and a fag in your mouth,
as thin as a rake. It felt like an act of commitment

to bury you, to dredge the moat around you deeper
and deeper, leaving your head exposed and smoke to rise.
I was kept ashore for safety, but wanted to wade back

into the glimmering – where light perched, it tilted and dipped.
Now I had a new mother, I thought, who'd taught me
the vitality of fear which felt like reverence,

I needed to do it well, tamping from end to end:
to bury my father, who snoozed, in a dolmen of wet sand.

Priest Skear

'Twenty three illegal Chinese cocklepickers drowned when they were caught by
the tide as they laboured for a pittance two and a half miles from the shore near
Boulton-le-Sands. Morecambe Bay is a treacherous place. The combination of fast
tides, quicksands, draining rivers, shifting channels and sheer unpredictability has
trapped the unwary for centuries. Horses, tractors and trailers plus the odd quadbike
and transit van have sunk slowly into the sands and never been recovered. At high
tide, Priest Skear is the last receding outcrop to vanish under water...'

The Guardian, 12 February 2004

I

They go down again, imagine them, spun
in a roaring vortex of gravel, spun

and somersaulted by the force of water,
burning water, hard in the throat and the mouth

as stones that hurt. The throat at such
a distance from each snarling man gulps water

and draws it in again. They are bound to each other,
all twenty-three, by whatever part of the human body

touches at any given second, like a system of branches
struggling in and out of – trying to climb –

what might be thought of as a trunk of light.
And they are bucked and thrown about, gulping

until their cheeks are buckled tin. They shed coins,
a Wellington boot, their eyes shrink back

into their heads, as if their lips are magnified;
until they are overtaken, overtaken

and the last lit up cellphone spins
to the bottom, spelling out *no network coverage.*

from *Priest Skear* (2010)

2

They go down. The sea tonight too immense,
too sudden, the speed with which it fills the night-cave

against all natural law, upstaging the red words
of its warning-boards. Consider the power-surge

of the tide, the tonnage of seawater bulging
between the points of the Bay so it can only rise

and rise, swollen as it is by estuaries
engorged by the floodwaters of two rivers

as volume combines with speed, speed with volume
to isolate Priest Skear. The tide comes in

quicker than a man can run, dislodges the hardware
in the depths of its quicksands it creates but

never in the same place twice. This is not a sea by which
to be surrounded suddenly, two miles out:

the maker and disguiser of powers
that pull you this way, dislocate your arm

and spin you and spin you around again;
that take your head one way, feet another.

3

They go down. Creating such a downward drag
they threaten to draw down with them the catcalls

and upholstered benches of the Lower House
into the plug-swirl, but do not. They drown

with one snarl. One snarl. One throat. The throat
the muscle flexing, trying to filter

the intake of sand, silt and weed
that will be found later in the airways, on the slab.

And when the filter can't work any longer,
when breath cannot be held, there is huge inhalation

of water, not air. The whole body draws
upon the heart's already taxed reserve and the pulse

slows down. The deep muscles of the neck
begin to haemorrhage, one rib, one vertebra

cracks. One filled-up glove is magnified
ten times its size; in two to three minutes, the heads drop

and the hair sweeps up, beneath an upstream of gas:
goodbye, goodbye, goodbye.

4

They come up, breath bursting. But for each body
that sinks slowly to the bottom of the seabed

another body swims out of it, another body kicks
itself out of each drowned body, and surfaces.

They surface, all of them; they make it to Priest Skear
as if its pile of rubble were the safest place in the world,

the last bit of dry rock still proud of the sea
to which they cling like a sail – a raft of survivors

exactly where many do not want to see them,
an embarrassment (new collective noun) of Chinese.

If it can cling, it can swim, and decides to swim
the mile or more from the sanctuary of Priest Skear

from *Priest Skear* (2010)   87

towards streetlamps haloed in mist. At which stage
the Englishman brandishing his specs in the air

as he is fed the news the Chinese are safe, are now ashore
and being treated for hypothermia,

sighs to his assistant – what a shame, what a shame, he says,
these little fuckers got so good at swimming.

5

They come up, gasping. Some rip off their clothes
so they can more easily fight for their lives.

They rip at their own buttons until they're naked,
more than naked, they rip a way to their nerve-ends,

to their neurons, to their bones. They go down,
they go down, but shed clothes which are drench-heavy

and set them adrift for the sea to play with:
for a while the clothes jostle each other – so bright,

some ripped, some buttoned, all twisted up –
until they themselves are separated by the tides

like bright sea-flowers, like Mayday signals,
and will be found by morning, some five, some eight,

some ten miles apart. This purple blouse
with a label still attached, with its arms stretched out

for the arms of Priest Skear. This drenched gilet, hung
by its arm-hole from Hollow Scar.

These yellow pantaloons, legs apart, hooked
around the pelvis of Haws Point.

6

They come up. *Priest Skear!* The launch's lamp-beam finds them
knock-knocking into one another, face down,

the nightmare flooded into consciousness –
they're hauled in by hooks, or hoiked aboard naked

as Priest Skear's last sinking metre of crag
sinks to fifty, to thirty, to twenty centimetres,

to two, to one, and is gone. Whatever died down there
and found its way to the bottom, then surfaced,

must weight the launch in the bows. What's sent back to shore
is a holdful of drowned men, but our problem is

the figures that wake out of them, that sit up,
throw off their blankets and now crouch on the deck,

warming their hands around mugs of soup.
Drowned men are never drowned enough, they say;

huddled under a single tarpaulin for warmth
they chatter out in mime the best of Babel's gibberish

and their knuckles are large, they're here for good,
and just look at the way they hold your gaze.

7

They go down. And the words they'll never speak
and which will never enter history, never be heard

and never recorded, also go down, go down,
go down, washed away as if never there.

Those vocal-chords full of stress-timed sounds,
of glides and vowels, plosives and sibilants,

from *Priest Skear* (2010)   89

those glottal stops that hook onto the larynx
like tiny parasites, and cling for dear life

along with the fifty thousand characters
currently fattening in the Kangxi dictionary or perched

on the tongue of Mandarin Pinyin – all of these
are thrown into chaos. Some of their vowels leap

onto the dry rock of Priest Skear, slither like fish,
the bull-whip of their bodies kicking to a halt;

others sink, like heavy books, into the depths.
The Atlantic consumes the lot. It swallows

their protests and accusations, their gags
and their grief, fear of reprisal, obedience. Their *cry*.

8

They come up. Thank God for the coastguard's ladder
lowered from the helicopter towards the ghosts

of forty hands which reach up from Priest Skear
and catch hold of the bottom rung at third attempt

and – whatever drowns below – haul their bodies clear
by clutching at any rope or foot or limb they can

like a great straining net of herring – so
embroiled are they and wrapped around each other

they drip and overflow as the coastguard tilts
and whacks, whacks, whacks away.

In such night and crawling sea-mist as this
the helicopter cannot be seen – just the throb

of engines passing through their bodies
as they're swung clear and smoke is whipped off the waves:

though they grip and they wrestle and climb up
over one another, placing a foot on the neck

of the one below, not one of them knows for sure
toward what these wobbly rope-rungs lead.

9

They go down. Though a force in these bleak waters
can spring up the shock of a dinghy – bright orange –

it can't compete, however hugely it inflates, with the vortex
which begins rotating very slowly

to drag down the Chinese but also drag down
their fourteen wives, sixteen mothers, eleven fathers

and thirty-six uncles, grandma times seven, ten creditors
and the Yuan they were owed, plus the dinghy itself

and these twenty homes collapsing in on themselves
in an avalanche of rafters and tiles and bricks

and two hundred items of discount furniture,
the dresser of white plates circling down in slo-mo

along with that wardrobe and upright grand,
these six cars made in Russia, eight pop-pop bikes,

these eleven crates of unpaid, final reminders
and letters from the dead in elastic bands,

two mistresses, four dogs, three quadbikes,
two battered pedal cars. One parrot named Tsu-Li.

10

They come up, like unlosable evidence, the drowned
turned greenish bronze, nibbled by crustaceans,

laid out in a row like two football teams –
the ligaments of the shoulder-girdle strained,

bruised and ruptured, aroused as never before
like something trying to break out of the body;

the monster of survival born in that moment.
Air in the shirt's back panel, ballooning, air

between vest and body, lifted up that weight;
their foreheads, their noses grazed by the sea-floor, the sea-rose

of a haemorrhage worn in the left ear,
each head ducked lower than the body to read

the depths, its slow hair moving in the calm …
each hand clutching something where it was torn off

from the world, fracturing the fingernails.
In their pockets, gravel, silt and sea-lice.

And neglect, like a shifty old ghost, turned to stones
that were tied to their ankles and wrists.

11

They go down. The winter current too strong
and their limbs not strong enough – this the physics

of the sea. The men who might have warned them
with more than a tapped watch and told them to turn back,

Arcimboldo's Bulldog

turn back, turn back and get their bodies out
in time before high tide on this moonless night

of pitch-black sea, of wind blowing force six,
are this minute in *The Lamb and Wolf* – practising:

here are the cornets, topmost voice for melody;
here the Flugelhornist puffing the solo seat;

here the Tenor horns and Baritones holding
a neutral bed of harmony, pitched high, less high,

the Four Valve Euphonium the pulling power –
As the Chinese go down, the band goes trembling up

and trembles, trembles to crescendo
with closed eyes, puffed cheeks, building around the deep voice

of the trombone pumping out like a heartbeat
the bottommost bass line of *The Keel Row*.

12

They come up. They come up. And with them surface
the last bits and pieces of a wrecked vessel

that might have gone by the name of *Albion*.
They roll over, so pale, when the tides attempt

to roll them over the other way. Find for us
the culpable, say their mouths full of darkness.

We drown many times, many times, they say,
we drown many times but never will drown.

We might be dressed in chains of bladderwrack
but these are our knuckles, and these are our hands

from *Priest Skear* (2010)

and these are our feet that are swollen with gas
and these our burst lips, and these our tongues

which though they are stone will continue to speak
of your gaunt minsters, all fingerclasp and itch.

The tides return, the monster's trapped in the harbour
and now it is the door-bolting rationales

shutting one after the other against the surge,
too soon, too late, too soon, too late.

Stigmata

'Today the Chinese gangmaster Lin Liang Ren begins a fourteen year prison sentence on twenty one counts of manslaughter and related charges for his part in the deaths of the twenty three cocklepickers who drowned in Morecambe Bay, February 2004.'
The Guardian, 24 March 2006

Now all the blame they expect you to take
x-rays straight through you and finds nothing there;
it passes through the weft of your overcoat and vest
and finds only these bone buttons, dark inside your skin.
And the salt-mark of the sea has reached your waist;
and the salt-mark of the sea has reached your chest;
and the salt-mark of the sea has reached your chin.

The salt of the sea though it might be blood
also leaks from the punctures, from the holes in your hands.
When the Atlantic thunders, it thunders through you,
while your pilot flame is tearing, tearing at its wick.
First you cup it in your palms, duck your blueish cheek,
then have your overcoat to shield it against the wind;
then try to relight it, relight it. One last match.

from *Priest Skear* (2010)   95

The Living and the Drowned

Thank God, or chance, for the geyser of steam
that burst from the boneshaker when it blew at last
and then ticked cool in the lay-by, laden as it was
with sneaked-in Chinese – a rocking lamp
casting them in and out of the dark.

A day from the cocklebeds, they were safe,
and news of that old van made it seem the dark hole
from which the story sprang, a torch
shone into the corner of my consciousness –
death's cubbyhole crowded with beautiful faces.

I thought how their heads might have flopped
into sleep's shedding of mistrust, rocked perhaps
by the motion of the van, then sprung awake
as the pistons locked up and juddered them to a halt
to separate what happened from what did not.

A bucket of moons scarfed in yellow, red,
a-flare in darkness, what might have happened
a future inspecting its ghosts – Thank God
for the breakdown which kept them from joining
the tangled drowned washed up by first light.

Thank God for the tardy, the finally stopped.
Other cabins of smuggled people
and similarly overtaxed pistons were that minute
tackling the steep waves of Pentland Firth
or the troughs of Cape Wrath, up and down.

Only the poor, the well-steered and delivered
get themselves to the mortuary drawer on time.

'...Sinking water, many many sinking water'

for Guo Bin Long

Every tragedy has a final word to speak,
and every final word has its sound turned down

first simply quieter, then quieter still,
every final word mimed with no sound at all.

While water reached his knees, reached his thighs,
while water reached his thighs, reached his waist:

the water at the waist, at the sternum, at the neck;
the water at the neck, at the chin, at the mouth

as he yelled as loud as he could, as he yelled into the mouthpiece
of his state-of-the-art, touchscreen phone.

from *Priest Skear* (2010)   97

The Gap Between the Boards of the Pier

The two bank notes floating down weightlessly,
overtaken at speed by a bitter rainfall of coins –
the purse fumbled, fumbled, the clasp undone

and disgorging the sum of your worldly fortune to
the waves – the sound of your wails above the sound
of the latest collapsing wave and the old pier-stilts

colliding below, down through the gap between the boards.
You were five, or less, and the forty metre plunge
that opened beneath your feet created a version

of the Atlantic which you never quite forgot:
it sucked you in and out, you thought, grew dark as oil
and made the pier-end creak in its joints in the gale;

it received your donation ungratefully, and never wept;
it brought close to you the terrible presence of *depth*.

from

The Storm House

(2011)

Like Slant Rain

Trouble is with inventing a language, brother,
when the only other person in the world who speaks it dies
you're left speaking to no one. This mouthful of words,

of fat verbs and vowels and cases and morphemes
that stammer from the lexicon under the tongue
is desperate to be used and anxious to be heard

and competes against itself for the room to speak –
It crowds out my mouth with the need to keep alive
every O in our intonation before it ends up

on the dump with the clicks of Hittite and Kulinic;
our words seem stranded and strangely marooned
now there's no one to read the other side of them.

No one to read them the wrong way round and still
have them make sense, say they are the wrong way round.
No one to say the old humanist's slanting hand

would not have wanted a mirror if he was the other side
but it's more necessary now, and I read in it:
lately, I confess, I've tried scrawling to myself in the glass

but, like any mirror-writing, it's slant rain. And like slant rain
it goes on falling and tearing, falling and tearing.
Like slant rain it quickens suddenly and slows down

and is heedless of its own expenditure.
Like slant rain it goes on falling and tearing, falling and tearing
and the glass does not know what it sees.

Calling Ugolino

Through what might be
the earpiece
or some grainier,
more primitive
instrument, brother,
or perhaps
the miracle
of the auditory
nerve, summoning
some signal,
a ruched pinhead
of decibels,
I imagined I might
be able
to hear your voice –
it would be faint
and strange,
belonging
as it does now
to another age,
the pauses
between it
prolonged by the whelm
of distance,
the static of water:
instead, the
soft voicemail
kicks in to say
you are
unavailable
to talk.
I had something
to say, I had
something
to say, I say
to the tape-hiss.

Arcimboldo's Bulldog

The Water-Halt

The *sshsshssh,* the chambery smell of the dark
were borne from room to room by the Chapel official
in sniffs, her sideways glances, even in the look
with which she turned out of the candle's blue-ringed circle

with over-earnest tact: the crucifix above your toes
offered proportion to sacrifice – its striped dazzling image
waylaying the retina among the shadows
when I confronted your final, fuck-it-all visage:

you might have sat up, brother, but couldn't slip
the shackle of muscles which almost secured
a smile, thumbed and moulded to reshape
the malleable substance – your grim composure.

And for the more, there was only less;
and for your brow a freezing, terrible kiss.

The Gorse Fires

I very gently drew out your brother's tongue
and placed it back again, said the coroner,
but began to feel it might have done it by itself.

Through the stethoscope, through the sternum,
he said, I could hear all the way to the sea bottom.
The eye with a torch shone into it – uninhabited.

What did he die of? That's the question I'm very glad
you've asked, he said. Ah, bodies – so many! Each one
more wiped, more stony-faced than the last,

pulled out in the drawer with a label tied to its toe.
Your brother might've died from drowning,
stroke, Septicaemia, a shot from a range of half a mile

or, to put it another way, he said, the common cold.
The liver's bloated gland sifting its silts of salt
like moraines, like pond scum. Or spots on a tonsil.

The puckered arc of rips, he said, ousting the flesh
of his back like a crescent of bitemarks
that might have been a hoeing of six-inch nails

but, you must understand, they're merely braille.
Some bodies, he said, catch hold of the lies of the dead
and must be slid, unkissed, back into the drawer

while the outer world bursts with lively evidence.
The gorse fires blaze across the moor and kissing is
in season. But look at his mouth when a square of mirror's

held over it – nothing. It reminds me of a sign saying *privé*
at the gates of consciousness where no one had
trespassed for many years. Look to the living, he said. They should
be kissed and kiss often and live to be a hundred.

Arcimboldo's Bulldog

Versions of a Miserabilist

One thought, from over the river: the mosquitoes
lost the smell of blood in me half way across.

Old Eden verity – I am no more to blame for my death
than I was for the sleazy rendezvous of my birth.

God alters selfish men – now that they have no face,
he has them regard the face, he teaches them how

they should have lived in a universe whose every centre is
a little pot of self-regard, a little like yours.

*

This is the end of money, though we have black fingers;
this the seedy afterlife of things. Everything poised,

as if the next step were already on stand-by:
like a star in the cavity the pilot light keeps

the steady job of incremental burning.
The meter wheel spins round and round towards

the astronomical bill that will never be paid.
These are your concerns. The fridge, my symbol,

persists in its puddle and on-off fugue. Just when
you think it is finally dead, it rambles to life.

The Law of Primogeniture

Whatever the planets were doing that second
they stopped, then resumed. The night
of the drop – the night of the touchdown

among the people he had chosen.
Mercury and the full moon conjunct
opposing Mars. The void preparing

to match his likeness against the world's.
Vertigo for the very longest descent
of all, and motion sickness, jet-lag

and homesickness drawn down into one
mix towards the imminent focus of
a yell. The great scarlet hollyhock opened

and opened until it could open no more,
until the pressure ripped it at the rim
and my brother came into the world head first

on a deluge of his own making,
swinging limp bloody fists as if he was inconsolable –
Mother, son, swim forever in that blood.

★

Later by six hours, though, crouched thoughtfully
over the day's eighteenth stooping fag-ash
which is held up by a sort of freakish gravity

my father is burning and poking the afterbirth
that crackles in the boiler like fat:
through the scorched glass he watches it burn yellow.

Though he shakes out the thought almost before
it skids beneath his thinning hair, he imagines
the afterbirth might be the sack

from which Rasputin emerged undrowned,
stones tied to his ankles and wrists.
So close, he squints into the flames' hysteria:

and he thinks his way back through
fag eleven, ten and nine, to where
he is running alongside the midwife's bicycle;

and he thinks his way further back
into the moment of conception, and imagines it
a single burning point of light;

he thinks his way back to the night he met her,
so overcooked with gesture – on the tilted floor –
so faux with shallow flirtation;

and he thinks his way much further back
through ten, through a dozen years
with giant stumbling, backward strides –

he stumbles back, muttering I must, I must
find a way back in time, in time –
out of the way you frowsty armchair –

you lamp, you flying – *fucking* – heirloom.
He stumbles backwards, like a man
doing backstroke with a chair in each hand,

a stool kicked out of the way by his right foot,
a pot kicked out of the way by his left.
He stumbles backwards, and just in time

(...against the timer's whirring) swings
one baggy trouser-leg over the other
and reassembles in the chair, from pieces, as the flash –

catching the lush valley of his parting
and good looks exploding in light –
goes off: *Me*, he whispers, *Me*.

Goose Flesh

She climbed with the weeping boy
into the sleeves and legs of his clothes. He crouched

and acquiesced, and what he thought was his hand
reaching to pat the soft part of his abdomen

was in fact hers – her foot was in his shoe – so it was hard
to fathom if those scarlet toenails belonged to him

or her, and which body musk seeped out
from which armpit, which thought originated first

in his head or her encompassing head behind,
so little the lapse, the spaces, between them.

When he dressed himself, it was her hands that reached
around to each bone button, her fingers which clipped

the absurd butterfly to his collar. When she climbed out
and left a chilly shape where she had been

he felt his spine was corrugated and exposed,
every follicle of him, every single blond hair

always listening for her approach,
listening in all directions, from every hair.

When she climbed back, he could no longer feel
the coarse stitching in the seams of his shirt

nor any sensation in his feet at all
and no sensation in his hands or in his lips.

Where her warm belly brushed against his sacrum
he smelt of her cologne, and it was only

when he tried to shift his shoulders sideways
and fidget his body into a space

that her long arms folded across him from behind
and drew him back towards her, at which stage

they seemed to wrestle together in a black sack,
one trying to keep the other where he was

by pulling the collar tighter against his neck,
one trying to escape from his shirt.

The Revenant

This the door
opening from
the back of my neck
like a hatch
on a hinge:
(...you are such
a furtive, shifty
and insistent
ghost – you use
the hatch
like a cat-flap.)
And this, brother,
your mewling
for food –
you expect
always to be
welcomed back,
while the flap
behind you
wipes out the last
of your tracks.
I must submit,
it seems,
to your taking
of death's steps
in reverse,
climbing the rungs
of my spine.
You climb so slyly,
so cagily,
as if to say:
where the ghost
comes to feed
through the hatch
there's a bowl.

Bucko in Love

The dog had the love, and gnawed it to the marrow,
absorbing it all. It drank love into the roots
of its unthinkable purple skin. There was a sense

of how love softened its ferocity and long tooth;
how it was turned cow-eyed and lugubrious;
how the love it absorbed became something else,

perhaps, a sort of pact, a covenant made
by the three who combed it, brushed it, fed it
and expected it to ingest their need.

Its whiskers wet with droplets of fog,
its wolfhound tongue slipped sideways
over the molars of its ancient grin. It secreted

the want of mother, brother and father
in its sweat-glands. They loved it so much, at times
it seemed the dog would swallow them whole.

It always answered, never spurned their attentions
or doubted it existed for them. It grew
three heads – one for each of them in turn,

and had no head for me. I knew it knew I knew.
I envied the dog for being doglike
and more worthy of love. I drew the saw's teeth

across its midriff, sprinkled it with hot water
so that it winced and cowered away.
Eating raw meat, acquiring a sense of smell,

trying to think of ways of hoovering in the dirt
and of developing unnatural tastes
at length I tried to become the dog

but it remained itself, looking back at me:
I dreamed its ribs creaked slowly apart
and opened like a gate on the garden.

Deleted Scene (The Frog)

The terror lived in the shed, we knew. It was the buckled mirror
propped in the depths, in which the frog grew smaller and smaller;

poor frog – it dried up so slowly in our tin's evaporating wet.
When death, like a stirrup pump, sent gasp after gasp puffing into it,

as its body withered, its eye-gold seemed to swell and swell.
Somewhere way inside itself, sucking at the rest, the plug-hole

against which it struggled to be froglike. It was like a little old man:
that wide-mouthed countenance suggesting a concordat with pain

or mere dumb incomprehension, while the spider on stilts of hair
stumbled over the nape of our necks and made us both shiver.

I left you crouched at the door, brother, when the shed's roof-felt
so pressure-cooked the terror, and grew so hot in summer, it'd all
                                                    but melt;

I left you crouched at the door once I had, considering how to, stepped
through the speckled sheen of frog and mirror in one step.

The step was long, and now you're dead, I find myself wanting to ask
for some primitive forgiveness – against the slit of sky, cirrus-flashed,

you were abandoned to a space less than half a metre square
and circled yourself repeatedly, or strained into the dark, from where

it was always high August and the door-slit bulged a brilliant fog
out of which you stooped and grew smaller, face to face with the frog.

The Brothers Grimm

There was milk though the dead had lost their thirst
and its shaken crates set off in early air
when we entered the chapel to find him
rouged in his long gown and coffin where

the big sprays were light and the hands of those
who wished to keep him with them got a grip,
and one of us took, one offered energy,
one kissed the brow which burned and froze his lip

and turned away, full of protein and iron,
out of the place in which the other stayed;
one of us took energy, took calcium,
one lay down smiling by his father's side.

from *The Storm House* (2011)

A Portrait of My Grandfather in Drag

When all those who do not wish to play with him are left at home
he steps into the storm, the free-for-all, of chromosomes;

the future's a movement of heat in the road – he so rouge-obsessed
we lumbering oafish boys might fear we'll never get to exist;

we fear he'll never get to fill the shoulders of his coat, or fit
the belt that here would wrap around him twice like a straitjacket.

He's an identity, he mimes through the storm, under construction
but for the time being is bits of self flung in all directions:

in Richmond, though, in what might be Nineteen-Twenty-Three,
or Four, it's lip-gloss, fan and feathers and bits that fly away

as the lippy girl, who so disturbs me, steps out of him to reveal
the forces perched precariously on that abyss-edge of stool –

I'm disturbed but curious and, through the magnifier, trace
the last centimetre of a hair that separates the uncle from the niece

and the niece from the angels. The flash explodes in the dark
and between him and it a daylight of reciprocated shock.

Look in any encyclopaedia. *Gender's* a river in Noord-Brabant,
a gong struck in Javanese gamelan music and the agreement

of noun and pronoun, but tonight, says grandpa in his billowy silk,
the rest is so much glazed and so much slippery talk.

Arcimboldo's Bulldog

'...Lay thee down'

It came back to me quite suddenly – carrying with it the curl
and doubling-back of undertow, things said
in ignorance and later forgotten –
the day the curtains, brother, closed you away

and we stood chewing grief like rinsed lettuce.
Every night for as long as you and I shared
that back room – I said it to you;
loving the sound of the words which played out

excesses I could never quite put to sleep,
I said it, over and over again:
for the last time now goodnight, Davy;
for the last time now goodnight.

from *The Storm House*

The only piece of action in the dream was the opening of the window, of its own accord; for the wolves sat quite still and without making any movement in the branches of the tree, to the right and left of the trunk, and looked at him. There were six or seven of them. It seemed as though they had riveted their whole attention on him.

Sigmund Freud, *From the History of an Infantile Neurosis*, 1918

2

Sequestered brother, a year dead, now the world
must get by without you. If once you had willed
world and self into being, and looked for their limit, now
the world vaporizes with the self. Let's say
you're further from home than me tonight. Out here,
estranged from my own life, I've the space to confer
with your rather untalkative absence. It might be
a sort of praying, or a speaking of terms which will
remove me further and further from the lobby:
the noise is far below, now that I've slipped away
and have to lift the dicky bar of the fire door
to retreat to my room, until a time rain through the glass
streams, like a ghost, over the hotel letterhead
which was never once intended to address the dead.

3

Untalkative brother, a year dead, everywhere world
is in the ascendant. Out here the air is heavy with rain,
the crowded lobby like a railway station.
Out here, estranged from world, I feel the urgency
to explain exactly what it was that happened to you
and to dig for the whole story, manhandle you back
into the frame and weigh you, measure you, thump
electric shocks into your body, smudge off
the mortician's make-up from your face and wipe away
all blame and false forgiveness. I want to rewind the flames
that flowered along your limbs, at finger and toe:
I want to walk you out of the furnace, put you together
as if by doing so I might be able to map
a way back for you, forward for me. Then let you sleep.

4

I want to suck back the hissing along its jets
like the flame-spirits forced to withdraw the flames
and find you whole, sit you up, winch you
in your collapsed kilos by your armpits and swing
from left to right the mickle hams of your fists:
I want to wrestle you back into the world and lift your chin,
so very gently, off your chest, detach the dark
lying close against the balls of your eyes.
I want to put you in shoes, stand you up, persuade
the tiniest buttons through your button-holes
and, after the journey, have you speak a few gruff words.
But look at the tongue – that giant glib muscle slumped
into speechlessness, less instrument than bung
and unable to tell us one damned thing.

from *The Storm House* (2011) 119

5

Talking to the dead's not easy. I'm robbed in daylight
of the gift of speech – any mouthful of words
as if cluttered out with stones impervious
to the seep of listening. Any word like a stone,
so smooth, so hard, nothing can soak into it.
Wittgenstein was right. A private language
is like the stone. I can talk of the birthmark exposed
by your hairline, those fingernails deformed
by years of chewing, but the stone absorbs nothing.
Whatever words I use are like rain that is yet to fall
responding to the shock waves of the thunder;
at the window, a dry spot in a future which rains:
along the ridge of the wall, moving fast,
the spun green and yellow dome of an umbrella is hurrying past.

16

When the pressure broke, almost like relief, the blow
you landed on the fragile pot of her skull
was of such force it broke the stick in two. Her vertebrae
contracted her just a little more, her ankles
hardly able to support what mass she still possessed
fell from under her, her brooch unpinned and flew off
like a panicked bird, she flailed as if blindly
then dropped. When she dropped, you might have dreamt
she carried the identical likeness of you
in that dying fall, since first you linked hands where
you sprawled on her sternum, and grew to four to twenty to fifty
without once letting go, as if it were no more
than fingers which welded the clasp
and sent roots thirsting deeper, into the dark.

The stick came down from every angle,
there were twenty, no, thirty sticks, each seen from another angle,
each coming down empowered by the reason
for its own force, more vehemence here for this
less vehemence here for that, some regret here,
some grief, some asking-for-forgiveness,
but in that moment, I do believe, most sticks imagined her
sat in a wicker chair on some Bolivian balcony
watching insects over water, comfortable she was too far
from her sins to be blamed. And the damage done
by the blow, you were convinced, was a kind
of suitable punishment, a sort of justice.
It was justice that was energy, justice that was fuel;
it was justice that put the whip in the ferule.

22

The most important conversation we never had
dug the deep hole it might have occupied when
I received the news, and spoke into the mouthpiece:
you've done it now, I said, you've done it now.
Up the wall, you replied, she drives me
up the fucking wall…oh dear, it is so very hard
for you, I interrupted … At which stage you hung up, hung up
and would never speak to me again, and I was left listening
to the dialling tone which had an ironic sort
of sing-song note at large in it, and the low growl
seemed to deepen and now continues deepening,
goes on deepening one year after your death
as if it is smooth pebbles knock-knocking together
in the cold, the wolfish belly of the river.

from *The Storm House* (2011)   121

You know the turnings beyond the world
that have never been mapped, the pathos of the last street lamp
getting smaller and smaller. You know the truth
of how light divides, how the world slips through
the finest division of light, and is gone.
You know the terror of the peacock which
legs it across the lawn, as the first drops of a million gallons
bounce a leaf, then another – this is how it begins.
The snarl is gone. The flood in the lane will gather
to overwhelm its defences and pick up silt
and the night release new mineral smells
which are cleaner and newer, fresher and more green:
water is air, earth water. Air is fire, and the fire
of water's getting hungry for its reservoir.

from

Madame Sasoo Goes Bathing

(2011)

The Flame Trees of Trous Aux Biches

Not wishing for a moment to be upstaged
by clouds of blowsy blossom that cannot stay
although they are the queens of death and sex,
although it's light that holds them in its net:

not wishing to be thought at all plain
on their highway diet of two-stroke and gasoline;
not wishing to be outshone or overlooked
by the brilliant and branch-outreaching, swept

by salt-wind toward the inland spaces, they –
as if many gases leaked away
then rose and then spread thinly out
like tresses, like coiffures of cloud

that hung on the air –
set light to their hair.

Darwin in Maritius

Of all the mysteries the elephant, he said –
on whose back he took a strolling drunken ride
south to examine rocks of elevated coral,
thrown gently from side to side, as light peppered
through the weft of his floppy brim under which
his squint face lost itself in beard and thought.
Just the straps creaking, creaking against
the creaks of the bamboo through which they strolled:
how was it a beast, he thought, ten thousand pounds in weight
with inch-thick skin much given to insect bites –
drinking each day some forty gallons through
the sixty thousand muscles of which the length
of its languid and free-swinging trunk was made up –
could freight him with so soft, so noiseless a step.

Madame Sasoo Goes Bathing

Mme Sasoo, sombre, but determined
to overcome her nibbling inhibitions
and have the warm Indian Ocean lick
at will about her body, does not undress, but dresses up

from ankle to neck in brightly figured rayon
and wears her manly shoes to wade
from shore of drums into the tilt of water
with elbows aloft, all her attention below:

she is not young, but bears herself
with subtle dignity, though her costume clings, grows fat,
as the weight of water starts to rock
against her, and bullies her from left

to right, so she is like a high wire walker
riding out the admonishments
of the deluge, with dogged composure,
holding that perfect crimson mark

in the middle of her forehead level
over the waves. At which stage, her doubts
regroup and call her back to the shore
where her towels, and Seiko, are safe

but every article of her nakedness
she wished the water could explore
and taste like expert tongues has been
stolen long before she dared to wade.

Arcimboldo's Bulldog

You and I feared the dark in the dog
but knew it was a curtain or a telephone.
Every time you said it wasn't pleased
to see me I said it just wasn't pleased.

Look, it wants to lick a face, I said.
We thought but did not say a word
of what it had licked in its days of grace.
When I kicked it out, it crept back in.

The steam on its breath, you said, oh,
look how it drips saliva on my foot.
Stepmother, though stray cats keep us apart,
these are the bits and electromagnets

of old devices and telegraphs, ear-
and mouth-pieces out of which we wired
the dog together and assembled it.
It was transmitter and receiver, good as new,

through which we strained to hear,
we strained to speak. The static *itched*,
itched in its ears. The dog was inclined
to grin more widely the deeper it scratched.

from

The World Before Snow

(2015)

Ommerike

We're told how a flight of grackles and cowbirds
dropped out of the sky in Baton Rouge, thudded
everywhere on the ground, blossomed into gardenias:

the like of light on all that wan and numinous yellow
had never been seen before. A rainbow jetted up
against a pitch black sky. In a single short stretch

of the entire Arkansas river, a million drum fish
flapped ashore. We are not dead, said the fish, we merely
change state, and some prefer to say that we are dead.

You're entering, you say, the new nature in which
anything can happen, where fish begin to swim on dry land
and you and I meet and fall, meet and fall...

this could be something we have done before,
each stoop, each step itself, some form of resumption
though the feet are longer, flatter, the feet are longer,

and what we carry, like a greeting, like old pain
kept in a ciborium that holds it as any sealed pot would,
cupped in our hands like a hawkmoth which beats.

Self-Portrait as Drag-Field and Dark

There was the dark in you, it hung over your features;
there was the dark I saw and recognised what it was;
there was the dark along the eye-line, the wilt of dark

like it had branded a mark from inside you blindly
onto your forehead, and settled all along your mouth;
it had settled all along your bottom lip, changed its shape,

as if to inflect your countenance however brightly
your hair flashed and you shone. The dark charged
to barter with the dark in me, you belonged to someone else;

you belonged to someone else, and so did I.
We were caught, it seemed, in the star's drag-field
which meant the room very slowly started to rotate.

What began was begun at the dun, customary table
where all things must begin. The id seemed to hug
to the dark that could not be shaken from the head, and dragged

you from your costly peace. Nose to tail, the dark
lay docile at our feet, where we sat and granted one another
the cheek of our best profile, lit from the same side.

Self-Portrait as Shamdeo Talking to his Future Self

Each fingernail grew like a creature yenning for a new existence,
arched, grew grimy and long, became a kind of implement;

I grew, I cleaved to the muckle of warm wolf-blood
and whatever sort of feather and down it actually was

the filthy nest was woven with – sorrow and ferocity.
Those two old antagonists, so much at odds, both riled

by how much of each they found in one another,
the cast in the eye encroaching like some sort of moon,

snapped and squeaked, and circled. They opened their mouths
as wide as they could but not a single word came out.

There was only their scrapping. And the gasp. In one,
in many, mouths. I could not talk. I was dumb with filthy hands

which bled from the stones, like my soles. Every longest step I took
was comprised of tinier steps. You stood me on two feet;

you said, from way way up here, *this is what you see.*
You read to me slowly from the excellent texts;

my grubby finger, its one trimmed nail, caught up with every word;
you taught me to gargle your vowels and consonants

and a mouthful of them both began to make a sound;
I was shocked by – afraid of – the growl of my own voice.

from *The World Before Snow* (2015)   133

Self-Portrait as Oxymoronic Love

We like to bite, so fierce that it is tenderly. We mime to wound and tear,
we grip to hold, with teeth. But do not wound or tear or grip or hold.

We like to bite so hard, so tender. We scrabble, we panic, smile
and relax, we balk, enthuse. We energise, withdraw, we make, are new,

there at the gate of being, where we live. It is an oven, a clock,
a thermometer. It is a gate now closed, now open. We will talk
                                        the kindly,

ravaged way to ferocity, the blissful walk from fierce, to happy.
Talk has no end, we know, but we talk our way to the end of talk,

gull-gasp with open mouths that are empty of sound.
Biting's the new talk. To kiss, to kiss and to bite, at once:

newly budded in want, our teeth that are lethal, are harmless,
are sharpened by want, are blunt, blunted. They scar, draw blood,

those tiny ring-moats are not ring-moats but marks of birth.
I only hate, forgive me, because I love you too much,

now sweet, ferocious-tender, fair and just, now bottoming in grief.
Your hands, diminutive, grow large when they induct

a solace that disturbs the nerve, comfort that bends us double,
reassurance that makes to fret, fretting which becalms. Oh,

we shout, we shout – grow furious – we kiss the shout to sleep!
We bring each other these offerings, one by one. Finding it among

a million smoother and more symmetrical on Einstein's beach,
you have gifted me a lopsided heart, like a stone.

Self-Portrait with Hummingbird as Fingers and Tongue

They might have a ruby throat, black chin, fly vortices,
they might be sleek aquamarine and weigh no more than a penny

and might have wings that whir at infinitesimal speed
as they hover at my ears – your diminutive fingers, your hands –

as if they're drawn by fructose and glucose and galactose
each of which could be sensed, smelt, while something drinks,

something drinks in mid-flight. Your fingers and hands
will hover there in mid-flight at my eyelids, as if little bits could

be nibbled from them when they're shut. So tiny, your hands
could be weightless, or the weight of them lifted by wings

that are so tiny and beat so fast they beat but cannot be seen.
They beat so fast, like a racy heart. They lift the weight

of your fingers until they hover at my forehead, peck;
your fingers, your hands are not heavy, but need the wings to lift them

to my ears, to my eyelids and to my forehead.
Your tongue, your tongue also has wings that beat so very fast,

that blur invisible though the tongue's foregrounded plainly,
it needs the tiny beating wings to lift, to lift the weight of it

until it touches my tongue's tip and hovers there like a beak
tip-tap-tipping on the window, wooing its own reflection.

Ommerike

The snowstorm came down, it blew across Boston,
it said all roads behind you are closed for good;
when mass collides with mass and crawls lower,

when snow falls for forty eight hours, you have to stop.
It blew. It billowed. Such weight of snow to stop
everything in its tracks. Stop, said the snowstorm,

set out, when I abate, from here. Stop, and watch
the whole of me blow in silence through the glass.
The tumbler knocked from the table by mistake,

it said, is yet to reach the foyer's marble floor.
The body of whosoever is dumped headlong
will fall but never reach the bottom of the well …

My plane touched down on time, your train was held up
which meant it got in as my plane touched down.
Some fluke of clockwork meant my chronograph ran

as many seconds fast as yours was running slow.
We were booked into the same room by clerical error
under the same name, which was neither of our names.

Self-Portrait as Old House Filling Itself with Furniture

The house, being cold stone, knew better than them how emptiness,
destitute of voice, had a single note which deepened. Only trees

in silence flailing at the windows, like an invocation, like a trance,
only a cloudy-tipped, sixty watt light bulb attempting to cast

the brand-name on the wall. It was afraid of its own ghosts,
the house, and seemed to dream the latest tenant who saw,

at the other end of the landing, a naked woman standing a moment,
who seemed as she walked towards him about the physics of future,

the sort of storm which followed her. At which stage, shelves
of books rose to the ceiling. A mirror cartwheeled upstairs and flew

to the wall, like the blinds. The great cupboard surged into place,
the couch finagled an impossible space. The bed-frame dropped

onto its iron haunches and thundered like a piano moaning,
settled in inertia. A clear night hatched. The Pleiades slashed

across the rooftop, so intense. The old house, in its own trance,
dreamt her appearance, across the narrow landing, hauled

a whole life into view, up out of past or future, or up out of both,
like it was wholly attached to her. There were pillows! There were
                                        pillows,

light as their feathers, falling and falling. They fell where they fell
into their place, her hair on the landing long. The lights in the cellar

came on. Forgetfulness, dreamt the house, will be
cured by forgetfulness. Insomnia by lying awake.

Self-Portrait with View of the
Greater Chihuahuan Wilderness

From this angle, you can pan over all those cracks in the ground
to zoom in, at very high speed, on the crack in his lip.

So this is the lip-crack itself, close up, roughly in the centre;
it is like two halves of a creviced heart and he lifts his finger to it.

What put him there? Oh, the horrors of the subjunctive.
What began as a *yes it is*, became an *it is not, is not.* As one truth

fell away, to reveal the half truth behind it, another truth fell away;
the untruth showing through the half truth showing through the truth.

When he looked at her, he knew he did not know what thought
lay behind the thought, or exactly what might be contained in it.

The wilderness opened. If trust was a crumbly levée
it collapsed and fell in and what poured through it was doubt pure

like air, like sand, like dust. What began as yes *it is trust*
became the wilderness, and he was stood on his own out there among

one-thousand-five-hundred square kilometres of uncertainty.
He thought of his thoughts, opening like cracks in the ground;

the extreme temperatures which begin to drop at night.
This may be a desert, but it overflows with wolves.

Arcimboldo's Bulldog

Self-Portrait with Flowershop Idyll and Nihilistic Love

Our love licks salt, cracks fleas. Plucks hairs. It knows the name
of each of its organs. Like this. It, being itself obsessive,

has its obsessives stroke the other's face, as if to figure out
what it is they stroke. It augments and it dignifies;

it excites. It, being itself tumultuous, has its recusants shelter
from the storm that clatters in the doorway when there is no storm.

Our love's renunciation. Lawless. Selfish. Hates everything
but itself. Like this. We are lost in the flashmob of blooms.

Attentive to each other, inclined to touch, to fondle,
we have hands in each other's pockets, hands in each other's hands,

talk in each other's mouth. Our love, being snarly and kept,
misleads the flowergirl; she thinks every word she speaks is heard.

It will, being hungry, have us as victims. It makes its victims not know
how strange they are, strange to others, not strange to themselves,

it has its victims bear perpetual witness to themselves. Like this.
It, being unkempt, doesn't know, they say, what damage it does,

what grace it earns, advice deletes. It, having a gorgeous smell,
                                        is effluvial
as this green gas, has a smell-less smell like certain orchids. It is thick

as baby breath, like tears inside a particle, particled in summer cumulus,
bottomless as flower-baskets, vacuous as flowergirls;

it, being turgid, in such turgid oxygen, among the lily-tongues,
the most extreme of specimens, bespectacled like this.

Self-Portrait with Goffstown Deep Black and Sun-Up Intensity

Black at its blackest. A town asleep. The only way to walk
deeper into the black where the weatherboard homesteads seem to rise.

I edge, like the blind, down the rainy incline which is a tunnel
channeling one thought to the end of it: leave her in this town.

Leave her among the quiet woods and the saturated grass;
leave her where some say she belongs, give her back her life, her family

and her shiver of trees now shedding their way to cicatrix
in the season she most adores, now black, black-leaved, black-boled.

Such dark can funnel you the decision when its walls are close
so *turn,* right now, turn right now, *turn right now* – to see above the town

such a vast ingot-ring hemorrhage out from the mountains and take away
your choice. It dents, it stabs, your pupils with its intensity. It says love

is the havoc at which you cannot balk. Take her out of this place
which holds her, stunts her, neglects her, a million miles from the world;

the sun's further off, over the gulf throbs in furious truth:
it says, know her, you have found her. Take her from this place.

Against the depths of black, it says, this the insistent brilliance:
it burns behind your sternum and it burns behind hers.

Self-Portrait with Mary Ann Lamb's
Akansas Toothpick

Mother, you lie at the source of the long black river
that does not love the world. You knit black shawls

at the very end of it. Your needles are ivory's shocked white.
Mother, you made yourself a necklace of unthinkable things

which jangle and clash, which knock and witter together.
You bid the Nibelung dwarves come to your knees

and they bob all around you, waiting for you to choose.
Mother, you clamp that caliper around the heads of those

who will travel up the river. This is how you assess them.
You scrooch over your own body like a bird, you pick up

a crumb from your lap. You watch your reflection
in the vague oval and dream it is someone more innocent.

Mother, you laugh, rock back, you have no teeth in your head
which is full of perished veins only, you claim, and little else.

You sit in this room, in the deepest of chairs,
wrapped in your shawls and chair-arms like a sunken fog,

like a ghost with a wide mouth. Mother, when younger,
you turned your head away against a cirrus-blowing sky.

Grunt

'Well…tell you what. Curley's like a lot of little guys. He hates big guys. He's alla
time picking scraps with big guys. Kind of like he's mad at 'em because he ain't a
big guy. You seen little guys like that, ain't you? Always scrappy?'

John Steinbeck, *Of Mice and Men*

Your foot shy of the rowing machine's baggy loop left by Babe Ruth;
his feet twice the length, three times the width,
that big toe, the left one, an embarrassment.
He was Six-two, weighed two hundred and fifteen pounds;
his length of arms have reached around you twice.
What he had in body, though, you make up for in subtlety,
in charisma, in wit and in charm, you think,
even though a hundred pounds lighter, even though five-eight;
when you row you grunt, as if to inhabit one bigger,
as if the bigger grunt might propel you like a sail.

It goes on, the war between big and littler men.
Okay, you say. The ghost goes through its work-out.
For its every long pull on the oar – from shin-bone to waist –
you have to pull five or more to keep up with the pace.

Self-Portrait with Hiss and Rattle of Sleet

Not frogs, not grackles or cowbirds, but sudden and tumultuous,
sleet – we're the only place for miles around, it seems, where sleet

does not fall: sleet hammers on, slides off, the umbrella, makes a space
that is dry. As much as it fizzes on the countryside, road

and every square inch we can see, it makes for us this space
in which we stand, hunch, lean-to, in which we huddle together

to watch sleet get more boisterous – it reaches our extremities,
it gathers like snow on our sleeves, our backs and our shoulders,

out in it: mesmeric. Compulsive. The way those little cuticles of ice
clatter and blitz, sizzle and rebound, parabola and skip.

Each one contains the storm. They jig and leap. In slow mo and real time
they act out their crazy ballet of expenditure like grapeshot,

pure pelletry, like blasted grains. Like maggots bouncing, you say,
they all come down and try to find themselves a little home.

They fizz and crackle, don't last long; it is their death-dance –
We huddle close, are strangely indoors, and can hear how sleet

can blast itself against the road and somehow make a tender sound.
There is more than rib and nylon between enfilade and dry,

between the road and the clouds. We talk with big voices to drown out
the hiss and rattle of sleet by which our voices are drowned out.

from *The World Before Snow* (2015)   143

Self-Portrait with Flames and Arapaho Bison

We should have taken better note of what crashed through the wall,
what primal animal force, head ducked, what near-extinct species

which can cross any river more than a mile wide from what to
                                                    whatever;
what force when drought-moulted, when smelling water,

sets a thousand like it running. Stuffed, it froze as it crashed.
In the bar beneath, though we hardly knew it, we were more taken

with the smell of burning, more taken with the flames themselves
– the bus back, burning in the black of the snowfield –

which might well have been the smell of preconception in flames,
the smell of chance, like rubber, burning. The smell of discretion,

like kerosene, burning up, then tearing in the wind. The smell
of neglect, like the stuffing of seats, burning. The smell

of stagnation, like the nap-pile over the crankshaft, burning.
We fed the flames with the detritus and napkins of weddings,

a marquee's striped canvas, doilies, whatever stuffed collapsing thing
sat upright for a while in the flames and then fell forward.

It is my conviction that night that we were burned alive,
for the briefest minutes you sat opposite, you flexed, you flailed,

you grinned so wide, you seemed like me to be fuel for flame,
all we'd been was eaten by flames which lengthened, which blued,

we stood up in flames that burned us alive but could do us no harm...
Above the bar like a train, or an engine stuffed with time, unhurt

by all those flaming Arapaho arrows skidding off its back,
the clumsy bison crashed through the wall, we stepped from the flames.

Self-Portrait with Aquarium Octopus
Flashing a Mirror

Where water, glass and light cut through each other, where one side
of the glass is underwater and the other is not, one cosmos

seems first to bisect, then kiss, another. Up against the steamy divide
the octopus explodes and collapses, explodes and collapses

in its soft hysteria of saying: it is compelled by will or ennui to be
wholly on display, compelled, like any extraterrestrial, to show itself –

This is what I've got, it says with every lunge, I'll show you all I've got
which you don't have, this head, for example, clumsily bashing glass

like a blunt-nosed angel's, a throb of plasma. Though many limbs flower
crazily from this eye-lens, it says, I don't know what it is I've got

but here's the centre, the centre where it is. And you a man, a woman,
it says, and you neither or nothing at all – a smudge in need of an apogee.

You don't know what I am or what it is you are, you do not know,
whatever you are, whatever you are, whatever you are.

Arcimboldo's Bulldog